A POWERFUL PROMISE

THE IVY LEAGUE INSPIRED SECRET IMPROVING ACCESS AND RECRUITMENT AT COLLEGES TODAY

STORIES BY COLLEGE ADMINISTRATORS AND STUDENTS

Published by Ardeo Education Solutions
ISBN: 9798720538705

ARDEO
EDUCATION SOLUTIONS

Printed in The United States of America

A POWERFUL PROMISE

CONTRIBUTING AUTHORS

Mondy Brewer – Vice President of Client Service, Ardeo Education Solutions; Former Vice President for Enrollment Management, Lubbock Christian University

Frank F. Brucato – Chief Financial Officer and Senior Associate Dean for Administration, Stanford Law School

Mike Frechette – Dean of Enrollment and Student Financial Services, Pacific Lutheran University

Rachelle Gasior – Vice President of Client Service, Ardeo Educations Solutions; Judson University LRAP Recipient

Jordan Grant – Associate Vice President for Enrollment Operations and Student Financial Services, Seattle Pacific University

Sean-Michael Green – Vice President of Client Service, Ardeo Education Solutions; Former Vice President for Enrollment Management, Albertus Magnus College

Greg King – Associate Vice President for Enrollment Management, Illinois Wesleyan University

Brianna Loomis – Assistant Editor, HarperCollins; Spring Arbor University LRAP Recipient

Keith Mock – Former Vice President for Enrollment Management, Faulkner University

Matt Osborne – Senior Vice President of Client Service, Ardeo Education Solutions; Former Vice President for Enrollment Management, Spring Arbor University

Peter Samuelson – President, Ardeo Education Solutions

Jonathan Shores – Senior Vice President of Client Service, Ardeo Education Solutions

Abigail Skofield – Administrative Assistant, Vineyard Christian Fellowship; Huntington University LRAP Recipient

Amanda Zielinski Slenski – Vice President for Admissions and Special Assistant to the President, Alma College

Carroll Stevens – Former Associate Dean, Yale Law School

Patrick Verhiley – Director of Missionary Disciples Institute, Marian University

Dave Voskuil – Former Vice President for Enrollment Management, Emory & Henry College

PJ Woolston – Former Vice President for Enrollment Management, Marian University

Stephen Yandle – Vice Dean Emeritus at Peking University School of Transnational Law, Shenzhen; Former Associate Dean, Yale Law School

EDITORS

Justin Gillmar

Sean-Michael Green

Erin Kelly

Marla McKenna

Peter Samuelson

DESIGN

Robert Voigts

TABLE OF CONTENTS

Dedication
  Jonathan Shores, Ardeo Education Solutions

Foreword
  Frank F. Brucato, Stanford Law School

PART I
THE CREATION OF A POWERFUL PROMISE

PART II
STUDENT STORIES

PART III

COLLEGE STORIES

DEDICATION

JONATHAN SHORES
ARDEO EDUCATION SOLUTIONS

T he year was 2013, and I was riding high! I had just finished my first full cycle as the Vice President of Enrollment and Marketing at a college in North Carolina. I was in Arizona to share my success with fellow enrollment professionals at a national conference. As usual, I walked through the exhibit area and struck up a conversation with a relative newcomer to the scene, Ruthie Wellhausen with Ardeo Education Solutions (then LRAP Association). Ruthie's smile and personality were infectious. She exuded professionalism, fun and a strong work ethic that made me want to be her friend. Ruthie invited my colleagues and me to dinner that night, and because of the qualities mentioned above, we all became fast friends. Right or wrong, I always made decisions to partner with a service vendor based on whether or not I could see the representative and their company as an equal partner dedicated to helping me and my institution. Ruthie fit that bill, and the college began working with her and Ardeo Education Solutions shortly after the conference!

Ruthie was always great at keeping in touch with me as a new client. She wasn't just curious about how things were going

ABOUT THE AUTHOR: Jonathan Shores is the Senior Vice President of Client Service at Ardeo Education Solutions. He has spent over half of his life working in higher education. He holds a bachelor's degree and MBA from Campbell University and a doctorate from Northcentral University. Jonathan is a proud veteran of the United States Air Force, where he still serves in a reserve component as a Chief Master Sergeant, the highest enlisted rank in the Air Force.

for the college I was working at, but she also wanted to develop the personal client/vendor relationship that is crucial in higher education services.

One day, out of the blue, she called to tell me she had terminal cancer. Heart-broken and devastated, as if Ruthie were a lifelong friend, not just a recent professional collaborator and new friend, we talked for some time about her outlook. As usual, she was upbeat about the blessings in her life and how she was certain she had always lived life to the fullest. To anyone who knew Ruthie, it was obviously true that she did live life at maximum capacity. Every day was a new adventure for her, and she set out with her smile and energy to make the world a better place. Ruthie not only called that day to tell me her health news, but she had also called to offer me an opportunity to come on board at Ardeo to take her place on the team. In the short time I had known Ruthie, up to this point, I knew that I had big shoes to fill!

I vividly remember thinking that I wanted to stay where I was because I enjoyed the enrollment and marketing work I did on the college campus. Even though Ruthie and I only knew each other for a little over a year when she called to offer me this opportunity, I felt like I owed it to her. Her exact words to me were, "Jonathan, I want to know I left it in hands similar to mine." How could I say no?

As Ruthie began battling cancer, I came on board full-time at Ardeo. She fought, and she fought *hard*. I mentally and verbally denied what Ruthie was going through, and one day even told her that she looked too good to be battling terminal cancer. The doctors gave her a month or two to live, and in true Ruthie-style, she exceeded their limitations by almost three years. Ruthie's spirit, perseverance, drive and soul continue to drive me to be the best version of myself. It is a standard and a way of working with others that has rubbed off on the entire Ardeo team. Ruthie's vision and life are something that drives us daily, and we are grateful to have had her in our lives, even if for a short time.

This book and the collection of success stories that clients have had in addressing the negative impact of debt in higher education and the positive impact of LRAPs are attributed to Ruthie's memory and spirit. She is in each of these stories and will be in every story we have moving forward.

Thanks, Ruthie. We love and miss you!

FOREWORD

FRANK F. BRUCATO
STANFORD LAW SCHOOL

F or more than 35 years, LRAP has been an essential feature of Stanford Law School's recruitment and financial aid strategies. Formally known as The Miles and Nancy Rubin Loan Repayment Assistance Program, ours is one of the nation's leading programs. As we created this program and worked with DC policy makers to change laws so reimbursements were not considered taxable income, we were always mindful of our impact on prospective students as they choose SLS, on our students as they made their post-graduation career plans and on our alumni as they mapped out their long-term opportunities. Our program is one of our proudest accomplishments, in that it enshrines the School's long tradition of enabling students to pursue careers in public service and government.

I salute Ardeo Education Solutions for developing its now well-proven program for undergraduate colleges. I also very much appreciate their invaluable technical assistance in refining our own LRAP. Ardeo, a sole provider, now serves more than 200 colleges and universities and as the following stories make clear, its partners' innovative LRAP usage ensures that institutional goals are met while affording peace of mind to students and their families.

ABOUT THE AUTHOR: Frank F. Brucato is the Chief Financial Officer at Stanford Law School and a Board Member at QuestBridge.

PART I

THE CREATION OF
A POWERFUL PROMISE

THE IMPACT OF A POWERFUL PROMISE ON MY LIFE

PETER SAMUELSON
ARDEO EDUCATION SOLUTIONS

M y LRAP* story begins on a sunny spring day my senior year of college, as I wrestled with my decision about where to attend law school. I wanted to go to Yale Law School. I had never visited there, nor any of the law schools I was considering, because I couldn't afford the travel. But I did not need to visit Yale to feel the attraction and mystique of its reputation.

However, the University of Chicago Law School offered me a substantially larger financial aid package, and I feared the much larger student debt burden from Yale was a big risk that would severely limit my career choices. I wanted the freedom to work for a non-profit. Ever since watching *Cry Freedom*, a movie set in South Africa during the late 1970s apartheid era—which is also where I lived as a child—I had wanted to work for a non-profit so I could help fight injustice in the world. That would be impossible

ABOUT THE AUTHOR: Peter Samuelson is the founder of Ardeo Education Solutions. The "powerful promise" discussed in this book enabled Peter to attend Yale Law School. After a brief legal career with leading law firms in Hong Kong and New York City, and then as a consultant with McKinsey & Company, Peter became an entrepreneur to bring the benefit of Yale's "powerful promise" to students attending colleges and universities across the nation.
*Yale's Career Options Assistance Program (COAP) provided the inspiration and model for Ardeo's Loan Repayment Assistance Programs (LRAPs).

with huge monthly student loan payments. Reluctantly, I paid my housing deposit at Chicago and began letting my dream of attending Yale go.

On this sunny spring afternoon, I decided to sit outside and take one last, long, leisurely look at the Yale Law School catalog and daydream about the classes and other aspects of student life I would miss by going somewhere else. I discovered a few pages tucked in the back of the catalog that I had not noticed before, which described an interesting program called the Career Options Assistance Program (COAP).

COAP had a huge impact on the direction of my life.

Yale Law School was promising to repay my student loans if my income after graduation was low. And just like that, I felt free. I could attend my preferred school. I could take out huge loans without worrying they would chain me to a desk at a New York law firm. I could work anywhere after graduation—including any non-profit doing any kind of work—and Yale would make my loan payments.

I enjoyed Yale Law School, learned a tremendous amount and made life-long friends. It was everything that an academic experience is supposed to be.

After law school, I had the privilege of spending more than a year doing human rights work and travelling around the world. I joined a friend in Sudan and began studying Islamic fundamentalism thanks to a generous grant from the Ford Foundation, and then, thanks to other donors, I spent time observing communist oppression in Vietnam and China, where my mother and grandfather had been born. None of that would have been possible if Yale had not generously paid my monthly student loan payments through COAP.

Looking back, I benefitted from Yale's COAP in three ways:

- I was able to attend my preferred school.
- I was able to choose my classes based on personal interest, without worrying about whether they prepared me for a financially rewarding job.

- I was able to do human rights work for a year after graduation, despite large loan payments.

COAP had a huge impact on the direction of my life.

Although Yale Law School was a great experience, I never saw myself as a lawyer. I soon left law to become a management consultant at McKinsey & Company, where I worked first in the New York office and then in the San Francisco office during the dot com boom. During that same time, I joined the board of the college where my mother taught English and journalism for years—and where I felt I had grown up on campus as a kid after leaving South Africa—which was then named Central College in McPherson, Kansas.

Central College was very different from Yale Law School. It was a small college, in a small town. Central had a faculty that cared deeply about the personal growth and development of their students. The school worked hard to ensure their students would be prepared not only to find a job and succeed professionally but also to succeed as good people—to be people who cared about others and who made their communities better places to live.

> **I believe strongly in the life-changing power of higher education.**

In one way, Central College was identical to Yale Law School. Yale Law School also invested heavily to attract and admit students, only to find out too many went elsewhere (more on this in Chapter 1). Similarly, it too faced financial constraints and could not increase financial aid without limit. I realized that both Central and its students would benefit from the same program that Yale had used. Offering prospective students a Loan Repayment Assistance Program, like COAP, would allow Central to increase enrollment while saving money on financial aid. That would be a big win for a small college with limited resources like Central.

However, this big dream had a bigger roadblock. Central College lacked the resources and institutional capabilities to build and manage a program like Yale's COAP on its own. I decided to find a way to help.

I believe strongly in the life-changing power of higher

education, and I wanted students not just at Central College, but across the country, to enjoy the same freedom COAP gave me.

To that end, I founded Ardeo Education Solutions in 2008 to provide that benefit to students through our Loan Repayment Assistance Programs (LRAPs). With the help of many people, including former Yale Deans Stephen Yandle and Carroll Stevens as well as former SallieMae Executive Vice President Paul Carey, we built a strong product. Our first client was Spring Arbor University. With the support of the then Vice President for Enrollment, Matt Osborne, and their president, Dr. Charles Webb, we soon increased their freshman enrollment by 18% (learn more in Chapter 7). Huntington University was the first to give LRAPs to all incoming freshmen, under the leadership of their President Blair Dowden, CFO Tom Ayers and Vice President for Enrollment Jeff Berggren. They enjoyed similar results, as we helped them grow enrollment to help manage financial challenges.

> **LRAPs are a strategic tool for good that both empower students and advance institutional goals.**

This book—written by college administrators and students—is a roadmap to LRAPs. In Part I, you will hear from two members of Yale's founding COAP team about how they came to create the program and why LRAPs provide a better model than traditional financial aid. In Part II, you will meet three LRAP Award recipients who will share how the program transformed their lives. Part III will take you from one end of the country to another, as you hear from 11 college administrators at 10 institutions about their successes, lessons learned, strategies tested and students impacted through LRAPs. By the end of this book, you will have a thorough understanding of how and why this Ivy League inspired enrollment secret is improving access and recruitment at colleges today. Each year, more colleges join in to give LRAPs to more students.

LRAPs are a strategic tool for good that both empower students and advance institutional goals. Since our founding, we have helped tens of thousands of students attend hundreds of colleges across the US, and we look forward to helping many more.

CHAPTER 1

THE BIRTH OF AN IDEA

CARROLL STEVENS
YALE LAW SCHOOL

T he LRAP story began over 30 years ago, out of stark necessity.

In the late 1980s, Yale University, located in New Haven, Connecticut, was facing several challenges due to financial decisions made in the previous decade. In fact, every Ivy League college had fallen into that same fiscal trap, overspending on their endowments rather than saving some of those funds as a hedge against future downturns. Inflation rose and investment values plateaued, plus operating budgets took a big hit. Campus infrastructure began deteriorating, and funds for programs and people stagnated. As a result, tuition and fees had to rise, and they did.

Along with its competitors, the Yale Law School found that as such costs rose, loans became an obstacle for prospective law students. The Juris Doctor degree is a seven-year commitment counting the prerequisite bachelor's degree, and aggregate costs over that length of time became daunting for all but a few. An ever-

---

ABOUT THE AUTHOR: Carroll Stevens is the former Associate Dean at Yale Law School where he co-founded the Career Options Assistance Program (COAP), a predecessor of Ardeo's LRAPs. Since then, he has been involved in numerous entrepreneurial ventures and has held governance and leadership appointments at six colleges and universities. He currently serves as an honorary Fellow at Regent's Park College at Oxford University.

increasing reliance on student loans became evident.

Law schools traditionally had made financial aid a low priority, but that needed to change. Interest in law was approaching an all-time high, and in response, more merit and need-based scholarships began to be forthcoming—to the limited extent that resources allowed.

> **The Law School was, at the same time, facing another dilemma. It was at risk of becoming less of a truly national institution.**

The Yale Law School had a comparatively small enrollment and a correspondingly low-tuition base, so net-tuition revenue was insufficient to support a big increase in scholarships, as was the endowment. The School was thus boxed in and forced to think innovatively.

For a good reason, the faculty was dead set against increasing enrollment, especially if it was primarily to improve the School's capability to increase student aid through redistribution. Raiding the endowment was, likewise, out of the question. So, what could be done? We needed a plan; otherwise, the School's relative position would deteriorate.

The Law School was, at the same time, facing another dilemma. It was at risk of becoming less of a truly national institution. Given their growing loan burdens, fewer Yale law graduates could afford to go to smaller cities and states around the country, where starting salaries were considerably lower. More applicants from outside the northeast were receiving full-ride offers from schools closer to home.

The Yale Law School had earned its distinctive reputation by producing US Supreme Court Justices, Presidents, Senators, Law Firm Founders and many other leaders from small town/small state America. And we were proud of the Yale Law graduates who went on to become leaders in regional cities such as Birmingham, Cleveland, Louisville, Sacramento and Nashville. Indianapolis was a prime example. In recent years Indiana's Attorney General, the state's Chief Justice and the President of Indiana's largest urban University were all Yale Law School graduates. Such a tradition deserved to be defended. As further evidence of this tradition,

Associate Justice of the Supreme Court, Clarence Thomas, came to the Yale Law School from Pin Point, Georgia, and began his career in Jefferson City, Missouri. President Bill Clinton hailed from Hope, Arkansas, and started his career in Little Rock.

Guido Calabresi, a law and economics scholar of international repute, became Dean in 1985. High on his agenda was the idea that if student debt could be sheltered in some manner, the School would have a first-mover advantage against competitors and provide greater peace of mind to its students than would be the case if we simply increased grant aid. He set a group to work on a solution, thereby creating a balanced approach: scholarship aid plus loan protection that would be sustainable over time.

> He set a group to work on a solution, thereby creating a balanced approach: scholarship aid plus loan protection that would be sustainable over time.

What would such an innovation cost, and how might that cost be borne? Could such a program be self-funding through internal savings? Dean Calabresi felt that donors would be inspired to support such a program after demonstrated success, just as they had supported scholarship aid. But that wouldn't happen overnight; first, we had to design and implement the program, prove its beneficial impact for students and the institution, and then engage with prospective donors.

And we had to act fast. We had a mission to secure and a legacy to protect. The School had always prided itself on a well-balanced student body in terms of demographics, personal circumstances and characteristics. Things were changing, though, and our future was approaching very quickly.

The state of Connecticut is known as the land of steady habits. Change comes slowly in such an environment. That culture infuses many of its institutions, and Yale, at the time, was no exception. Given this backdrop, we knew when we made our case for approval; it had better be airtight.

I was new to Yale but had been an Associate Dean at the

University of Kentucky College of Law for more than a decade and had served as President of the National Organization of Law Schools and Legal Employers. So, I knew my way around legal education, including program development and fundraising. But my experience had been at a public university, where tuition at the time was still nominal. The specter of large-denomination borrowing had not yet hit my radar. But not long after taking up my new post, I had an awakening.

The occasion was a hosted lunch for the Dean of a Chinese law school interested in learning about American JD programs. I arranged for us to meet at a proper New Haven restaurant and invited a second-year student to provide an added perspective. Our discussion was wide-ranging, and most of his questions covered topics very familiar to me. But as our conversation came to a close, our guest turned to the student and inquired if she'd gone into debt to meet her law school expenses. When she said, "Yes," he asked, "How much?" At this point, everyone in the restaurant leaned into the conversation. Then came the student's reply, "$100,000." A collective gasp was expressed, my own being the most prominent.

> It was what we had to do if we were to remain competitive for the best talent while staying true to our egalitarian traditions.

I was instantly convinced we had work to do. The safety-net the School had created for student loans, for me, became imperative. It was what we had to do if we were to remain competitive for the best talent while staying true to our egalitarian traditions. From that moment forward, this budding initiative—a comprehensive loan repayment assistance program or LRAP would have my full attention as Chief Development Officer.

By no means was it certain that the University would approve Yale Law School's proposal for such a pioneering program. At the time, no such resource existed anywhere, let alone at Yale. Its financial durability could only be hypothesized—proof of concept having never been achieved.

My stablemates Associate Deans Stephen Yandle and Jamienne Studley had been working on the plan for some time, and at his previous institution, Steve had actually piloted a limited version. With the School's blessing and with the aid of a group of advisors, together they shaped the model that, in time, inspired the Ardeo program. Though it was entirely foreign to the University's thinking and directly contrary to the prevailing policies, approval was eventually given. (It's important to note that in the 1970s, Yale had launched a "tuition postponement option" similar to today's income-sharing agreements. It had gone badly awry, and the wind-down had cost the University a considerable sum financially and even more in the way of alumni goodwill.)

Our new LRAP, which we named COAP, for Career Options Assistance Program, was formally launched in 1989. Though its financial model was sophisticated, its core premise was straightforward and could be readily understood. The School would cover

The effect on recruitment and placement was immediate and transformative.

100% of financial aid applicants' needs, partly through grants and the rest through loans. And after graduation, one of two things would happen. Recipients would either choose a high-paying profession, in which case they would have the means to repay their loans or choose a lower-paying career, and the Law School would help cover their educational debt based on their income.

The effect on recruitment and placement was immediate and transformative. The School was once again able to live within its financial aid means. Its students were liberated to study what they desired, and as they graduated, they were free to pursue careers they felt passionate about rather than merely chasing the largest paycheck. Overnight our admissions yield turned entirely around, and we bested all of our competitors. Before COAP, two of three students admitted to the Yale Law School failed to enroll; after COAP, only one of seven did.

Most importantly, our traditions were assured, with students from smaller colleges, lower-income families and a more significant number of states once again vibrantly in the mix. Interestingly enough, one such example is that of Ardeo Education Solutions' Founder, Peter Samuelson.

COAP came to Peter's attention while visiting one of our competitors, and he was about to accept their very generous financial aid offer, which greatly surpassed Yale's. But in taking one final look at the Yale catalog, he found the section describing COAP and quickly realized its relevance to his desire to pursue human rights work. He instantly knew that COAP would be worth more to him than the grant he was offered, and he was free to turn it down and instead attend Yale—his first-choice institution.

> **Over the past decades, COAP has remained an integral feature of Yale Law School's financial aid program, and it has become a keystone to the School's reputational distinctiveness.**

Peter later pursued his human rights work abroad and subsequently worked for major law and consulting firms. After becoming a board member at a college, he believed that a COAP-like safety-net should be available at other institutions. Through a supporting organization serving many institutions, the necessary financial and logistical backing could be provided, sparing individual colleges uncertainty and risk. With the financial support from a few other stalwart believers, Ardeo Education Solutions was launched in 2008, originally under the eponymous name The LRAP Association.

Over the past decades, COAP has remained an integral feature of Yale Law School's financial aid program, and it has become a keystone to the School's reputational distinctiveness. Its gains in student yield helped make the School even more attractive to promising young faculty, which enhanced its already lustrous reputation. By the time the *U.S. News and World Report's* rankings were developed, and ever since, Yale has been awarded the number one position among law schools.

Just like at Ardeo client colleges, COAP was quickly understood and embraced by aspiring students and their families. To be sure, there were many memorable conversations at first, ones in which parents would refer to their child's multiple full-ride offers from other schools. Once they came to realize how COAP worked and what a Yale education would mean long-term, they would endorse their child's decision in Yale's favor, almost without exception.

In time, a group of individuals stepped forward to give in the $100,000 - $500,000 range, and that provided the confidence that an endowment supporting COAP could be created. It all took a bit of donor education, of course. Many at the time simply were not aware of the student debt overhang and how it affected decisions and outcomes: where to enroll, what courses to take, whether to follow one's head or one's heart when choosing a career path, where to locate and when to start their family. But, like me, once they heard student testimonials about COAP's importance, they were all in.

The very first appeal we made ended up being one of the largest COAP-related gifts the Yale Law School would receive. A husband and wife, both highly accomplished professionals, planned to bequeath all their holdings substantially to the Law School but were uncertain how it should be used. Their minds ran to a scholarship endowment to ensure that exceptional students could attend Yale regardless of their means. The Law School's representatives introduced the then new COAP initiative into the conversation, but the presentation was greeted with polite acknowledgment. It seemed clear their original preference for scholarships would stand.

Several members of the class, including civil rights lawyers, leaders in public interest organizations, small firm practitioners and people the class was incredibly proud of, spoke of being beneficiaries, a fact widely appreciated by one and all.

The School would check in with the couple from time to time, giving updates on overall progress and reporting specifically on trends in student life. Hints about COAP, of course, would be dropped. Such information was always taken in stride, with little feedback other than nods of general approval. They were people of few words, decorum and discretion. There was never an indicated change in their thinking.

Ultimately the pair passed away in close succession, and when their affairs were settled, their magnanimous gift was revealed and could be used for either scholarships or loan repayment assistance, as the School wished! Our request was fulfilled, and our dreams came true.

Others followed suit, with gifts made across the School's entire financial aid portfolio with no evidence that any facet gained at the expense of another. As for the Law School's overall fiscal health, there remains clear evidence that the financial commitment COAP represented was a wise one. The unrelenting pressure on grant funds was relieved, and as they became graduates, our students embraced the contribution to the shared ethos that COAP represented.

The first graduating class to be eligible for COAP benefits set an all-time record for a 25th reunion gift.

The first graduating class to be eligible for COAP benefits set an all-time record for a 25th reunion gift. It was clear from conversations at their reunion dinner that COAP was something they liked best. Several members of the class, including civil rights lawyers, leaders in public interest organizations, small firm practitioners and people the class was incredibly proud of, spoke of being beneficiaries—a fact widely appreciated by one and all.

The discussion about means and methods of student support took an especially favorable turn, for the Class of 1954, in part to the benefit of COAP. The Class Chairman, an inductee into the Venture Capital Hall of Fame, asked that we compute the value of $100 if invested in the Yale endowment in 1951—the year the class entered law school. When it turned out the figure was $15,000, he parlayed that to the scholarship recipients in the class and pointed out that Yale would be far richer if Yale had invested in its own endowment instead of in them. Yet again, the School enjoyed a record result from the ensuing gift.

It isn't only students and graduates of the Yale Law School who salute COAP's impact on student well-being. One of the program's original advisors, Robert J. Shiller, Sterling Professor of Economics and Finance at Yale University and recipient of the 2013 Nobel Prize in Economic Sciences, stated in his celebratory address to the campus that COAP was a "particular source of pride for Yale."

It was a very positive contribution to the student loan crisis.

Running a Loan Repayment Assistance Program independently is a formidable task for a single institution, even one with the resources of the Yale Law School. Successor Deans to Guido Calabresi have had to expend a lot of effort in keeping the program intact and viable. From time to time, adjustments are made. Like all innovations, a first adopter faces any number of challenges, some known and some unknown. The beauty of Ardeo Education Solutions, as a provider of LRAP, is its turnkey solution that spares partner colleges the work and worry of developing and maintaining a secure program. The program is almost infinitely customizable. The financial backing is ensured, high-quality client service comes without cost, student approval rates are above 95% and the claims process is entirely in Ardeo's capable hands.

> COAP was a "particular source of pride for Yale." It was a very positive contribution to the student loan crisis.

CHAPTER 2

USING LRAPs IN TIMES OF FINANCIAL CONSTRAITS

STEPHEN YANDLE
YALE LAW SCHOOL

B oth traditional need-based and merit-based financial aid are inefficient methods of allocating financial aid dollars, because they both rely on a student's current ability to pay rather than their later ability to pay. The effect of both need-based and merit-based systems is that they under- and over-award students. This results in significant discontent among students and their families and produces a return on large financial investments that are less than optimal for institutions. Loan Repayment Assistance Programs (LRAPs) provide a better model than traditional financial aid.

First, let's look at need-based scholarship assistance. There has been a long-standing noble commitment on the part of colleges and universities to provide needed financial assistance to make it possible for all admitted students to have a realistic opportunity to attend.

ABOUT THE AUTHOR: Stephen Yandle is the Vice Dean Emeritus at Peking University School of Transnational Law – Shenzhen. He developed and managed the Yale Law School Career Options Assistance Program (COAP), a predecessor of Ardeo's LRAPs, while serving as Associate Dean there. He holds a law degree and a bachelor's degree from the University of Virginia.

It is rarely possible for even the best-endowed institutions with the deepest commitment to access regardless of financial situation to fully fund their aspirations. As a result, need-based scholarships typically must be supplemented with educational loans and part-time employment to meet the full cost of attendance.

For many students from precarious economic backgrounds, educational debt, even that which could reasonably be expected to be paid off from post-graduation earnings, is a serious deterrent based upon firsthand family or community observation of the potentially crushing economic consequences. A modest amount of part-time work is reasonable to undertake. However, some students from lower-income backgrounds take on more work to decrease debt, and in so doing, undermine their ability to reap the educational opportunities before them and enjoy the experience. Whether their financial constraints are real or perceived, under-awarding results in many students electing not to attend or having a diminished experience if they do attend. Faced with resource constraints, schools cannot give an ideal need-based package to all who would qualify. If they give less aid to more students, they decrease the percentage of students who will choose to attend. While giving more aid to fewer students may increase the percentage of better funded students who would elect to attend, the effect would reduce overall enrollment numbers. Attendance among applicants with financial need who receive little or no aid would elect not to attend as a consequence.

> A more thoughtful approach would be to look at ability to pay as a "moving picture" that not only considers current ability to pay, but also future ability to pay.

At the same time that allocation policies under-award, they also over-award. They may have succeeded in attracting the student, but many students who graduate with little or no debt become financially successful and could have paid off higher educational debt quite painlessly after graduation.

The underlying problem is financial need is determined by current ability to pay. That is determined primarily by a look at current parental and student financial resources, a financial "snapshot" from the moment school bills are due. A more thoughtful approach would be to look at ability to pay as a "moving picture" that not only considers current ability to pay, but also future ability to pay. Thanks to the benefit higher education bestows, many with limited current resources will have high-paying post-graduation opportunities sufficient to pay off loan debt. Conversely, some graduates, for deeply held personal and professional motivation, will be drawn to careers with lower-income expectations that would make loan repayment difficult or impossible. The financial aid office has no crystal ball to predict a student's path to guide allocation of in-school scholarships.

Education is an investment that in most cases pays a substantial lifetime return. When we fail to recognize the lifetime ability to repay the investment, we over-award to some students and effectively occupy dollars that could have helped to address the under-award problem; however, it is difficult for either the individual or the school to know on the front end who is going to do well financially in their lifetime. The risk aversion of both the student and the school fuels the current inefficient financial aid system. There is a better way, but first let us review merit-based scholarship.

> **Education is an investment that in most cases pays a substantial lifetime return.**

Traditionally, colleges and universities have awarded scholarships to attract students they predict will excel academically. While the notion of reward for hard work and academic excellence viscerally resonates, there is a long-standing critique that merit scholarships are a zero-sum game for education. At high cost to schools, the same students merely move among institutions, not adding to the overall numbers who will attend. Regardless of the legitimacy of the arguments, merit scholarships are a dominant part of the competition for students. Most schools seeking selective student bodies feel they must compete in this arena or lose ground to competitors. Here, too, merit scholarships are inefficient as they are typically awarded based on past performance as a predictor of future performance. While there is surely a good correlation between past and future academic performance, it is far from

19

perfect and many are the cases of high scholarship students being outperformed by low- or no-scholarship students. Again, we see under-awards and over-awards with the over-award problem increased when the awards are decoupled from financial need. The ensuing discrepancies between academic performance and merit grants can create a resentment among those not receiving merit scholarships who out-perform scholarship recipients. That may well have an adverse impact on alumni giving among this group by fostering a belief that they have already "paid in full."

So what is the better way? A number of years ago the Yale Law School, wrestling with these thorny problems, decided to change the playing field and created a financial aid program contingent on post-graduation income. The school determined what it thought was a reasonable amount of post-graduation income. It then applied that to educational debt repayment and guaranteed that all students would receive post-graduation financial aid to pay the difference between what had been determined a manageable contribution from the student's income and the actual debt repayment. Below a certain income level, the student's contribution was zero and the school covered the entire cost of repayment. The school awarded no merit-based financial assistance and met the difference between educational financial need and available current student and family resources with a combination of need-based grants and loans. While the loan portion was high—but manageable without school assistance for students in high-paying positions—the repayment formula and the school's guaranteed portion were clearly stated and understandable. While an economist might argue it makes economic sense to offer only loan repayment assistance, parents and students have come to expect financial aid award dollars so a school that abandons the old model altogether would do so at its peril. That said, the blend of grant and loan can surely be adjusted with the addition of a loan

LRAP enabled the Yale Law School to assure students from low-income backgrounds that the school, not the individual or their family, would be responsible for repayment of the debt if post-graduation income were low.

repayment commitment.

LRAP enabled the Yale Law School to assure students from low-income backgrounds, that the school, not the individual or their family, would be responsible for repayment of the debt if post-graduation income was low. To the student who had been awarded an attractive merit-based scholarship from another institution, Yale could say after graduation that which the student might have borrowed at Yale in place of a scholarship awarded by the other school could be paid off painlessly from a comfortable income or paid by Yale as a post-graduation scholarship if the graduate's income was not high.

Numerous conversations with students confirmed LRAP was the decisive factor in their decision to attend, even in the face of large scholarship offers from other prestigious schools.

Creation of LRAP allowed Yale to use its financial aid resources much more effectively, and it substantially increased yield on acceptances without increasing total outlay for financial aid. Numerous conversations with students confirmed LRAP was the decisive factor in their decision to attend, even in the face of large scholarship offers from other prestigious schools. Given the high percentage of students who borrow to meet the cost of education and the fact that all students were eligible for the Yale program, students widely felt the school was providing a broad-based benefit and supported the program enthusiastically whether they ultimately took advantage of it or not. It has been a popular recipient of alumni contributions, in large part by students who did not receive program funds.

Because of the contingent loan repayment exposure, accounting convention requires large reserves calculated to cover the contingent liability of the program be encumbered. While Yale was in the unusual position of being able to self-finance the program, few institutions are in such a position. Most schools need an intermediary to develop a mechanism that allows those with lesser endowments than Yale to do what Yale did for itself.

Ardeo Education Solutions offers interested colleges and universities such a program that will permit them to increase access and increase tuition revenue without the financial uncertainty and the large encumbered financial reserves that would otherwise be required. I was so impressed by the careful and thoughtful financial planning and modeling that makes their program workable that I was moved to become a member of the Advisory Board for the program. The program brings to any school the opportunity previously enjoyed by only the most highly endowed few.

> **Ardeo Education Solutions offers interested colleges and universities such a program that will permit them to increase access and increase tuition revenue without the financial uncertainty and the large encumbered financial reserves that would otherwise be required.**

What is particularly noteworthy is not only does LRAP offer a sound and viable financial model, it is easily malleable to fit the individual needs and priorities of each participating institution. There are myriad possibilities for how an LRAP can be integrated with traditional scholarship assistance. Schools can elect how much post-graduation assistance is the right amount for their unique population. A cost that reflects a maximum value point for the school can be calculated to guide planning and decisions.

As the cost of education continues to rise and economic pressures mount, the promise of opportunity and fulfillment for students through higher education is in danger of becoming less real. Higher education must keep this important American dream alive, and one way is through maximizing the effectiveness of the dollars committed to ensure access to higher education.

Since I first wrote about how LRAPs provide a better model than traditional aid in 2009, the debate surrounding the cost of higher education has significantly intensified, and there has been a chorus calling for federal assistance to alleviate the problem. In recent political campaigns, there have been enthusiastic advocates from major federal programs ranging from forgiveness of existing student loans to "free" tuition. Unfortunately, all of the assistance programs that have received attention fall prey to the same inefficient over-award and under-award problems outlined earlier in this chapter. In aggregate, across higher education, the cost for this inefficient expenditure becomes staggering in magnitude —measured in trillions of dollars. Even if the expenditures were sound, it is an undeniable reality given the already massive federal debt. The bill will be paid by the American taxpayer, most likely in future generations.

Fortunately, it is not necessary to take such draconian steps to address the core concerns. There is a real under-award problem in that the price tag currently on higher education is a deterrent to students from lower-income families. The longstanding Pell Grant program was designed to address this problem with means-tested grants to make college affordable for all, but the Pell Grants have not increased at the same pace as the cost of college. The federal government already has loan repayment assistance programs that can provide significant help to students whose income is mismatched to their loan repayment obligations. Unfortunately, these programs are marked by confusion and mistrust. Many wonder, "Will the program end with the next change of power in Washington?" Federal programs can be part of the solution (e.g., a well-structured Pell Grant program), but it is highly likely that real solutions will have to come from the schools, not the government, as the government is too much in debt, too politically gridlocked and too poorly equipped to develop the type of fine-grained solutions that are needed. Fortunately, schools have a powerful and affordable tool to solve the higher education affordability problem—LRAPs.

> What is particularly noteworthy is not only does LRAP offer a sound and viable financial model, it is easily malleable to fit the individual needs and priorities of each participating institution.

PART II

STUDENT STORIES

CHAPTER 3

MY DREAM COME TRUE

BRIANNA LOOMIS
SPRING ARBOR UNIVERSITY

M y LRAP story begins with a dream and ends with a dream—quite literally. You see, ever since I was 14 years old, I wanted to become an editor for a publishing company. The movies I watched and the stories I read starring protagonists who lived in big cities and worked as editors and writers made the profession look glamorous. However, I didn't base my dreams of becoming an editor off of Hollywood's scripted narrative. My dream came from a lifelong passion of wanting to help people tell their stories. We've all heard the phrase, "A picture is worth a thousand words." While this is true, I wanted to use my passion for editing to help the literary and publishing communities show the world how a thousand words also create a picture.

I started researching publishing houses, following literary agents and authors on social media, and saving information about publishing internships when I was in high school. Doing this helped keep my passion and excitement alive—it gave me hope. But there was one inevitable part of this journey I needed to consider, and that was college.

ABOUT THE AUTHOR: Brianna Loomis is an LRAP Award recipient and currently serves as an Assistant Editor for HarperCollins Christian Publishing. She has spent the last four years working in editing and is passionate about helping authors tell their stories. She holds a bachelor's degree from Spring Arbor University.

I had always planned on attending college after graduating high school, but I was unsure how I would pay for it. My parents made too much money to qualify for financial aid but not enough to pay tuition. Sure, I applied for scholarships and had some college credit from AP courses I'd taken, but I knew I'd have to take out student loans if I wanted to go to college. And if I wanted to see my dream as an editor materialize, college was a must.

As I approached my senior year of high school, I was set on going to Michigan State University. Well, there was a brief moment when I was adamant about attending college in Alaska. I love winter, and I wanted to live in a place where winter arrived early and lingered the longest. But I think I knew deep down that was never going to happen. MSU was a happy medium for me, so I planned to attend there, study journalism, and experience life on a big campus. Plus, I grew up rooting for the Spartans. Green and white were my favorite fall colors and having grown up just an hour north of East Lansing, MSU felt like the natural choice.

For the first time since I had realized I was going to have to take out loans, I had hope for my future—for my dream.

My brothers, however, enjoyed their small, private colleges, and I was encouraged by friends and family to check out small liberal arts schools as well. I stumbled across Spring Arbor University (SAU) and remembered my cousin had great things to say about this school. It had a charming name, and it wasn't too far from my hometown. Plus, the English program looked fantastic. As I researched SAU, I came across this new program, LRAP (Loan Repayment Assistance Program), which was promoted on their website. Intrigued, I read every article, blurb and small print that mentioned the program, and for the first time since I had realized I was going to have to take out loans, I had hope for my future—for my dream.

I decided to complete SAU's new student interest form, and within days I received a call from my Admissions Representative. Over the next few months, I chatted with them about the school, freshman expectations, dorm life, the English program and LRAP.

SAU seemed like a great school, plus LRAP sounded like an amazing opportunity for me post-graduation. It seemed too good to be true, but as a person of faith, I also believed it was an answer to my prayers. All plans to attend MSU ceased, and I gave SAU my full attention. Funny enough, I applied to SAU before visiting the campus. I just had a feeling I was going to like it, and a few months later, when I went on my first campus tour, I confirmed this. It was a cold, rainy day, and to be honest, the campus seemed pretty dull. The rain and cold temperature probably didn't help, and it was also an early Saturday morning. Most students were still in bed, giving the campus a—well—sleepy vibe. I liked it, though. It was quiet, charming and small—all things I never knew I would enjoy in a school until that moment.

Knowing I would have help paying off my loans after graduation motivated me to keep going.

After the tour, we found ourselves in my Admissions Representative's tiny office, and this is where I learned of my acceptance into the school. It was also where I had my first in-person conversation with someone about LRAP. I don't remember a lot about that conversation, but I do remember, much to my parents' surprise, it was real. They were impressed, and I was excited! SAU no longer seemed sleepy. I was one step closer to fulfilling my dream, and LRAP was going to help me. I just knew it.

When people would ask why I chose Spring Arbor University, I had a list of reasons ready that always ended with LRAP. I could tell those listening to me were skeptical of LRAP and the likelihood of receiving loan repayment help. "How is that possible?" they asked in disbelief. They hadn't heard about the program. I didn't care, though, because I knew everything about LRAP, and it gave me the motivation I needed to accomplish my dream. If I worked hard, networked, did an internship, and got good grades, my chances of getting a job in my desired field after graduation were good. And if that happened, I would qualify for LRAP. Knowing I would have help paying off my loans after graduation motivated me to keep going. Every late night in the library, long day in class, numerous hours researching internships—it was all worth it because I knew I was going to be okay after graduation. I would achieve my dream without crippling debt.

I spent my last semester of college in Chicago, where I interned for a non-profit that published children's stories. I loved it, and I learned so much about editing, publishing and business. With just a few months left until graduation and no secured job offer, I started looking for jobs all over the country with only one rule in mind—a full-time job in my field. By April of 2017, I received a job offer as a copy editor for a small non-profit in Colorado. It wasn't an editor position at a publishing company, but I never expected to obtain my dream job right out of college. I knew that would take time. However, I was thrilled with the job offer that would provide me with editing experience and advance me one step closer to my dream. I accepted the offer and began emailing the team at Ardeo. I wanted to double-check that I still qualified for the program (with my new job), and after I spoke to some of the friendliest, most helpful LRAP team members, I acquired the information I needed. LRAP was going to help me pay my student loans.

> I remember receiving my first LRAP check in the mail. I cried. I laughed. I jumped up and down with joy! I was filled with extreme gratitude.

I remember receiving my first LRAP check in the mail. I cried. I laughed. I jumped up and down with joy! I was filled with extreme gratitude. While I had found a job in my field doing what I love, I owed more in bills every month than what I made. Making a little more than minimum wage while also trying to pay loans and monthly bills seemed nearly impossible. You know what did make it possible, though? The LRAP check I received every three months. Because of my LRAP success story, I became a huge advocate for LRAP. I encouraged my college friends to check it out and see if they qualified. And when my friend, who was a year behind me in college, graduated, I talked her through the LRAP process. I wanted everyone to experience the financial peace I had post-graduation, and LRAP helped do just that.

Thanks to the mobile deposit, I still have the first check I received from LRAP. I'm not sure why I've kept it so long? Perhaps

I've saved it for sentimental reasons, or maybe I just have some hoarding tendencies. I don't know. I do know that every time I rediscover it, I am filled with instant thankfulness and joy. I'm not exaggerating when I say that without LRAP's help, I could not have kept working in that copy editor position. I would have had to move home where there was zero chance of finding any work in my field. And if that had happened, over time, my dream of becoming an editor would have died.

I've been here for two years, living my dream, and when I think back to how I got here, I owe LRAP an enormous thank you.

Remember how I said my LRAP story begins with a dream and ends with a dream? Three years later, I'm writing this from my home in Nashville, Tennessee, where I work as an assistant editor for a large publishing company. I've been here for two years, living my dream, and when I think back to how I got here, I owe LRAP an enormous thank you. Thank you for helping me keep my hopes alive and for making my dreams come true!

CHAPTER 4

THE LIFE-CHANGING IMPACT OF LRAP

ABIGAIL SKOFIELD
HUNTINGTON UNIVERSITY

It has been 10 years since I first started the daunting process of discerning what to do with my life and where to learn how to do it. Even before the search began for the "right" university, my heart felt drawn to ministry settings to serve communities through church resources and social services. After graduating high school, I spent my freshman year of college at a small university in my hometown, where I focused on early childhood and special education. At the time, I thought teaching was the best way for me to serve communities, but something was missing. After just one semester of my freshman year in these two programs, I realized this call to serve others was still deeply impressed on my heart; however, the university I was at did not align with my values. I felt stuck in a place where professors didn't know their students and where I couldn't discuss my long-term vision. During my winter break, I attended a conference on social justice; my heart was hooked. I was determined to find a better way to serve my calling.

ABOUT THE AUTHOR: Abigail Skofield is an LRAP Award recipient and a 2017 graduate of Huntington University. Abigail has spent her career thus far working in various capacities, all focused on serving those within her community as well as communities around the world. Abigail holds a bachelor's degree and a license to teach English as a second language.

I finished my freshman year at that college, and my church invited me to spend part of my summer break in China. I received my first dose of traveling overseas and teaching English as a second language (TESOL) on that very life-changing trip. It spurred in me a desire to teach outside of the American school system. I knew I needed to transfer to a different college, but I had somewhat limited options because of how nuanced my hopes were. I wanted a rigorous program centered around faith, culture and a close-knit community where I could find a sense of belonging. Remembering the names of universities that might offer this, I unpacked an old box and began to revisit some of the letters I received during high school.

I painstakingly realized that my family could not afford this University.

As I sifted through that old box of college letters I had accumulated just a year prior, my attention drew back to a small university in northeast Indiana—Huntington University. Their message was compelling, humorous and evident on what they could offer me for my cross-cultural work vision. Initially, I had never considered leaving home for college, but I scheduled two campus visits with hopeful expectations. During these visits, I decided to transfer to this small, religiously-affiliated liberal arts University. I began my sophomore year majoring in cross-cultural ministry and teaching English as a second language. The very fact that I could pair these two topics of study together already made the visionary parts of myself come to life. Leaving my family and my sense of belonging in Ohio was still not something that came easy, but I was drawn to a place where I could hone my craft and develop my skills and passion for people.

As I look back on my HU visits, I can still recall what sparked that sense of excitement in me. I vividly remember sitting on a green couch outside a cozy-looking classroom, in the building where I hoped to be challenged and transformed. That day, I spoke with a man I hoped would become my professor and advisor one day. I was captivated by that place. Huntington University had a community genuinely centered around faith and a program where I saw myself thriving. I was given a folder that laid out the courses I would take there; each one was sprinkled with photos of smiling students partaking in all of the University's quirky traditions. These classes offered space to glean from PhD holders, interact with world-travelers, and develop my own thoughts about theology, culture and the world. I recalled the very first letter HU had sent me and how it communicated their values with humor and sincerity. I quickly knew I wanted to be part of everything this place was, and all it had to offer. It felt like home already— after just one visit. There was warmth at HU, unlike my first university. There was transparency in what they could offer me. There was a glimmer of hope at finding a new place to grow and call home.

LRAP could change our way of thinking about a seemingly expensive university. This place could become a feasible option for my family and me.

As we sat with my future professor on my second visit to discuss logistics, he laid out the numbers, and I painstakingly realized that my family could not afford this University. (I'm sure that's why I put their first letter in that box. I thought I couldn't afford HU.) I couldn't bear to leave this dreamy campus with its rigorous programs and close-knit community. As the conversation continued, however, he began to explain the details of something called LRAP. I'm not overly detail-oriented, so my parents and I asked many questions so we could understand the value this program added to my hopes of attending HU someday. This Loan Repayment Assistance Program wasn't something I had heard of at my previous university, nor did I initially believe it was as good as it sounded. I felt like I was missing the catch, but as he continued to explain how everything worked and what would be expected of me, it was really worth considering. Furthermore, I asked all of the same questions to the student giving us the campus tour and again to the Admissions Counselor. Every person conveyed the same information. LRAP could change our way of thinking about a seemingly expensive university. This place could become a feasible option for my family and me.

I knew the field I wished to step into would never offer much financially, but that never seemed to discourage my spirit or deter my family's support. Once the numbers became real and we saw how fast they added up, it felt like there was no other option than staying at a school where I wasn't thriving. We had already found ways to make a college degree affordable and doable there, but it still lacked so much of what I wanted and needed. None of the other universities I had considered during the initial search offered any loan assistance upon graduating. My teenage, melodramatic-self felt a little hopeless with such a daunting decision. I worked several part-time jobs and had no understanding of how to think about such big numbers or how to manage the intricacies of all things related to financial aid. LRAP made the difference. LRAP made things feel more straightforward and possible. LRAP gave my father the boldness and confidence to support my endeavors—even still. LRAP made student loans become less of a monster and something much more manageable. LRAP caused me to say "yes" to Huntington University, and I was full of hope for my future!

> **LRAP caused me to say "yes" to Huntington University, and I was full of hope for my future!**

During my last three years of college, as part of the Huntington University community, I traveled to three continents and worked in many different schools and churches. I met my soon-to-be husband from the other side of the world and learned new things that have forever shaped who I am and how I engage with the world. I became one of the students participating in some of those quirky traditions. I became one of the student leaders who brought others into the sweetness of the community. I became more confident and capable of going forth with purpose and being the person I was created to be.

In the years since I graduated from HU, I have continued to do social justice work in various countries. I've held several positions aligned with loving those marginalized and differently abled, and experienced the lifelong joys of community that came from my years at Huntington University. I continue to experience the value of LRAP. I've been freely generous because I know that I have assistance with my monthly student loan payments. I have been able to tell others about my alma mater and their partnership with LRAP for their students—for the sake of my family and me. I have prioritized what's most important to me because I have less worry concerning the limitations that naturally come with student loans.

Had LRAP not partnered with my alma mater, I would never have been able to afford a short-term trip with my church team to serve refugees in the Middle East. Nor would I have been able to return to the southern part of China for another summer to teach English. Had LRAP never been an opportunity for me, I would not have spent three years of my life mentored, taught and challenged by some of the most world-changing people. My alma mater offered me life-changing experiences that have proven invaluable, and none of them would have been a realistic possibility for me if I did not have the gift of loan repayment assistance. Now, I can pursue the tasks that bring me so much joy, including traveling overseas for ministry work, planning my two weddings in America and South Korea, and giving to causes that are dear to my heart. I can do all of this with confidence because I am not limited by dollar signs or strapped with debt. Sitting with displaced refugees in a shanty home or across the table from a student struggling to express herself are the moments I am made for. I have a sense of freedom to say "yes," which validates the goodness of this opportunity.

> My alma mater offered me life-changing experiences that have proven invaluable, and none of them would have been a realistic possibility for me if I did not have the gift of loan repayment assistance.

Becoming part of the team that receives this life-changing benefit had its fair share of paperwork and questions, but the fruits it produced have been far worth it. With every email I have sent to Ardeo, I've quickly received patient and thorough responses. When I've been out of the country and slow to submit for assistance, they were agile in helping me. I was supported as a student by attending informational meetings, and I have been supported as a graduate. Amidst the busyness of post-grad life and big-life transitions, receiving quarterly assistance has been a pillar to rely on; it has influenced my plans to move overseas and get married, as well as how I have stewarded my finances since graduating. It is a joy to me, knowing I can confidently continue giving to those causes, to help my family and future family pay for my weddings—to know

I am taken care of. The impacts of LRAP are innumerable, and I hold so much gratitude for each one.

CHAPTER 5

HOW LRAP KEPT ME ON THE RIGHT COURSE

RACHELLE GASIOR
JUDSON UNIVERSITY

L ike many, I grew up witnessing stress, exhaustion and frustration due to financial debt. These emotions played a huge role in the impending doom of "student loans" that consumed the early stages of my college journey. I was not interested in applying for hefty student loans, and private loans were incredibly daunting. The devastating stories and experiences shared by the media alone established a strong distaste early on.

During my senior year of high school, I decided to attend our local community college to pursue my associate degree. I am the middle of five children, and watching and following my sister's similar path was the most familiar route for my family. I knew it was up to me to finance my college education, and (like so many 18-year-olds) I was not committed to a specific career path, which made community college an even more appealing decision after high school. It allowed me to explore different classes while working a full-time job until I felt confident pursuing a specific

---

ABOUT THE AUTHOR: Rachelle Gasior is the Vice President of Client Service at Ardeo Education Solutions. She is a proud graduate of Judson University where she was awarded LRAP as a student, which empowered her to finish her undergraduate degree.

field of study and career path.

After my first couple of years at community college, it was time to restart my college search. I looked at many different types of institutions. I visited large public universities where so many of my friends were attending, near and far from home, and some that were much smaller. I participated in a college group at my church, where I first learned about Judson University, which was quickly followed by an onsite visit. I had no doubt, it was exactly what I was looking for: small, intimate community, staff and faculty that knew you by name, far enough from home to feel independent, yet close enough to drive home on the weekends if I so pleased. I would even be able to play for Judson's new Women's Golf Team—something that wasn't on my radar! Even more importantly, I found great interest in pursuing a career in Teaching ESL and met with Judson's Dean of Education. She instilled confidence and assured me I'd be able to graduate in two years. There was only one hold up. How would I afford it?

> I honestly did not want to leave Judson, but at the time it felt like all the cards were stacked against me.

I quickly shared my financial situation and concerns during my initial conversations with Judson's staff. Paying for my education would solely be my responsibility. Co-signers would not be an option, and I didn't have savings. Great start, eh? Fortunately, Judson's financial aid office was incredibly helpful and clearly outlined my options. I knew this was something I was willing to work for. After several weeks of conversations, paperwork, brainstorming and calendar juggling, I finally had my master plan in place. I'd make Judson a reality, and with confidence I would select the best payment plans suited for my needs. I would not take out any private loans.

My master plan consisted of joining Judson's Women's Golf Team (for which I received a partial scholarship), enrolling in a full-course schedule and eight-week practicum at a local elementary school, working two part-time jobs on campus during the week and working 20+ hours over the weekends to earn enough money to cover my monthly tuition payments.

As one might imagine, this "amazing" plan quickly fell apart. As I approached the end of my first semester, I was burning the candle at both ends. I was exhausted, contemplating changing majors, envious of all my friends who could do what they wanted on weekends/evenings, and it quickly felt like none of my dreams were worth it. Is this really what college was supposed to feel like? I had gone home for Christmas break feeling defeated and mentally prepared to change my plans, which included transferring elsewhere. I began looking at the local state universities where some friends attended. Financially it made so much more sense, even though a large campus and social scene was not what I wanted. I honestly did not want to leave Judson, but at the time it felt like all the cards were stacked against me. I needed a sign that Judson was really where I was meant to be.

> When I doubted everything (my career path included), this was the affirmation I really needed.

While I was home on break, I received a call from a lady named Ruthie who worked in Judson's financial aid office. She had seen that I pushed through the transfer paperwork and called to hear my story for herself. She wanted to understand my challenges and why I was looking to leave. It was an emotional conversation; I felt like a quitter but was at a loss for what else I could do. We concluded the conversation, and Ruthie told me she would go back to her team and see what they could do. I felt heard.

That same week Ruthie called me back—a phone call I'll never forget. She said she wanted to offer me an LRAP and went into great detail about LRAPs. She took the time to really help me understand how private loans work and how it would allow me to continue pursuing my degree at JU. I honestly couldn't believe it. Immediately I felt reassured, validated and at ease that this was the "sign" I needed. After further reviewing the details of the program and having a few conversations with my family, I felt an inner peace knowing that if I wanted to make this work, taking out additional loans would be worth it. More importantly, with the support of an LRAP, taking out additional loans would be far less intimidating.

When I doubted everything (my career path included), this was the affirmation I really needed.

Excitedly, I signed up for LRAP and had a new plan to press forward. I was even able to gain the support of two family members to confidently co-sign on these new private loans—an act I'll never take for granted. I vividly remember these conversations eliciting shock over the value of an LRAP and how it would assist me. They were eager to help me with this additional layer of protection and allowed me to confidently move forward with this new plan.

> A tool like LRAP can allow you to follow a career path that fills your bucket each day.

It feels like only yesterday that I was going through the job interview process during my final semester with such a profound sense of confidence because of LRAP. I truly felt that I could be more specific in my search and take my time finding the "right" first job for me after graduation. Those first few years of post-graduation are stressful enough, but the LRAP program gave me a sense of relief for my future.

Ruthie went on to join Team Ardeo and helped build it from the ground up. She shared her first-hand experience with colleges and families across the country and then offered me a position in the Company. Her passion was contagious and her spirit infectious, winning the hearts of so many of our early adopters. She infused her positive, cheerleading spirit into our culture and made sure everyone fell in love with LRAPs as much as she did. Over the past several years, I've had the pleasure of sharing my story with students and families all over the country. I've also been fortunate enough to meet so many others like me who have experienced the life-changing effects of LRAP. In a world with so much uncertainty, this valuable tool has truly empowered so many students to pursue their dreams and attend their first-choice college with added confidence to step out into the real world.

I hope my journey inspires students not to fear opening up about their financial situation. If you're willing to work hard and commit, then institutions want to help you succeed. A tool like LRAP can allow you to follow a career path that fills your bucket each day. And to all the college Administrators out there, take a chance on the transfer kid.

PART III

COLLEGE STORIES

CHAPTER 6

INVESTING IN THE MISSION

GREG KING
ILLINOIS WESLEYAN UNIVERSITY

I n 2017, I accepted the Dean of Admissions position at Illinois Wesleyan University. After working in Admissions for both the public and private higher-education settng for 10 years, this career move provided me the opportunity to work at one of the country's top 100 liberal arts universities. I was also able to work with, LeAnn Hughes, a former colleague who had been recently selected as the Vice President of Enrollment and Marketing after a nationwide search. Our common strategic and operational approaches and our commitment to embracing innovations and emergent technologies has led us to much success. We've adapted to the changing winds of higher education and have chosen to make a difference in as many students' lives as possible. When we were introduced to LRAP, we knew it was an extremely valuable tool. We thought, *Bring it on! Let's change lives!*

Before I dive into our LRAP story, let me tell you a little about IWU. Founded in 1850, Illinois Wesleyan University is steeped in deep history and has withstood the test of time while meeting the students' career-focused, experiential learning and liberal arts

---

ABOUT THE AUTHOR: Greg King is the Dean of Admissions and Associate Vice President for Enrollment Management at Illinois Wesleyan University. After nine years in public and private admissions in the southeast, he joined his colleague LeAnn Hughes, Vice President for Enrollment and Marketing, at IWU. Greg holds a bachelor's degree from King University.

curriculum needs. Offering over 80 different academic programs, including a School of Arts that boasts Emmy, Grammy, Tony and Oscar award winners and nominees, IWU also boasts a robust NCAA Division III and CCIW athletic experience. With a student to faculty (91% doctoral-level) ratio of 13:1 and an average class size of 16, the student population benefits from the extensive personal attention they receive.

The strength of IWU's commitment, combined with an actively engaged and supportive alumni network, has created a value proposition resonating with students across the state of Illinois and beyond. IWU is conveniently located between St. Louis, MO, and Chicago, IL and less than 200 miles west of Indianapolis, IN, in Bloomington, IL. Known as one of "America's Best Small Cities" by *Best Cities*, the Bloomington-Normal area provides two lively downtowns with a vibrant music and arts scene as well as parks and athletic trails running throughout the region.

The University's sticker price and packaged cost of attendance is often larger than our competitor market.

IWU's many other accolades include an annual first-year retention rate in the low 90% range, a social mobility ranking in the top 7% of the nation as well as higher average starting Illinois salaries. The return on investment at Illinois Wesleyan annually ranks among the highest in the country, as noted by *Kiplinger's Top 50 Higher Education Values*. The value statements associated with Illinois Wesleyan University demonstrate a tangible return on investment for prospective students.

However, the University's sticker price and packaged cost of attendance is often larger than our competitor market. In the top 10 cross-applicant list of schools, you will find several Big Ten institutions and a few very well-known private schools in and around the Chicago area. With a tuition, room and board price tag of just over $60,000 per year, even "top value" can be difficult for families to understand. Even though 92% of our graduates will complete their degree in four years, which will keep costs to a minimum, historical data states they will successfully enter their career or graduate school within six months at a rate of 97%. Sometimes that just isn't enough to convince families to make this investment.

We were faced with the challenge of demonstrating to prospective students and families that their decision to attend IWU would be validated in four years when they achieved significant success. Many don't immediately grasp that the long-term investment IWU offers outweighs its initial costs. We also needed to show the value IWU provides to families—with an Estimated Family Contribution less than what they feel they can pay—is worth the financial leap. A significant percentage of IWU's admitted students face gaps between their financial aid package and the total annual cost covered by student and/or parent loans. Even at an institution with a loan default rate (the percentage of students who cannot pay their student loan payments) among the lowest in the nation, these fears and concerns are valid for families and a significant consideration for institutions like IWU. This comes at a time when the value of higher education faces increased scrutiny regarding the benefit of the investment.

> **We were faced with the challenge of demonstrating to prospective students and families that their decision to attend IWU would be validated in four years when they achieved significant success.**

Adding to that pressure, student admissions in Illinois are incredibly challenging. The high school student exodus to other states is one of the highest in the country. Combined with increased recruitment nationwide within Chicago (more than 100 schools nationally have an Admissions Counselor working in and around Chicago), these factors have created an environment where the number of colleges and universities vying for student headcount far outweighs the supply of students. Even for small, private liberal arts universities with high rankings such as IWU, there is added pressure on pricing and discounts to meet institutional enrollment goals. The cost of private education is questioned, and a liberal arts degree isn't as highly valued as it once was. We often hear families tell us, "You are the best fit, and we are confident that our student would have a great experience here, but we're going to save $5,000 a year and go to state university."

So, we explored the idea of using LRAP as a tool. Would it be the deciding factor for those families right on the cusp of choosing an educational experience they would otherwise not be able to pursue?

The answer has been a resounding *yes!*

In March of 2018, we made our first LRAP offers to admitted students. Roger Kieffer, Vice President of Client Service at Ardeo, explained this to me a few months earlier. An offer of a Loan Repayment Assistance Program could be the difference in a student feeling comfortable committing to an institution rather than choosing to attend another, less expensive option. This option to participate in the LRAP program was another "tool in the toolbox" that conveyed the IWU education value and provided actual tangible proof to prospective students that the investment and outcome aligned. I could finally hear a student saying, "This school believes in their experience enough to invest in this protection for me!"

> **This option to participate in the LRAP program was another "tool in the toolbox" that conveyed the IWU education value and provided actual tangible proof to prospective students that the investment and outcome aligned.**

I had met Roger 20 years earlier when he was the Vice President of Enrollment Management at my Alma Mater, King University in Bristol, TN. I gladly accepted his call and welcomed the opportunity to learn more about this valuable new tool. As we began our partnership, Roger, along with, Sharon, the Director of Client Service at Ardeo, visited our campus to explain the LRAP opportunity to our Admissions Counselors. We could not be more pleased with the training, product updates and customer service provided to our students and faculty. In three years, each of our Admissions Counselors have approached me with a well-deserving student, and said, "I think this student would be a great fit for LRAP." That is a tribute to the excellent training from Roger and the entire Ardeo team. We have seen it make a difference with students and families in a variety of situations. Of course, our CFO wanted to ensure that LRAP attracted the students who would not have chosen us without it. No CFO wants to make an additional investment in a student who was already going to attend. Both Hughes and I knew this could be another step in connecting to students who had felt the investment in IWU was out of reach. Might we have a new tool that helps us create socioeconomic diversity in the class?

As enrollment managers, our inherent nature is to move to headcount and ROI success immediately, but did we not all choose this specific path to make a difference in individual lives? Rather than focusing only on our team's achievements and the institution, please allow me to share stories of best-fit students who might not have benefitted from all that IWU has to offer had it not been for LRAP. The Mission Statement of IWU speaks to a commitment to diversity and social justice. LRAP has given us a tool to better live out that commitment.

> **The Mission Statement of IWU speaks to a commitment to diversity and social justice. LRAP has given us a tool to better live out that commitment.**

In the spring of 2018, I met Samantha. She had a stellar application and, as time went by, proved to be a perfect fit for Illinois Wesleyan. Many institutions recruited Samantha, and she had many great choices at different price points. She explained, "I knew that IWU was the best school for me, but I had a hard time walking away from some of the full-tuition scholarships that had been offered."

Samantha had one more hurdle that troubled her parents, and it all revolved around her major and career aspiration. She aspired to be a writer and knew the IWU English Department would serve her well, as this department has prepared many writers to launch successful careers. I remember her parents asking, "What if she gets off to a slow start in her career?" And, "We can't quite cover all of Samantha's tuition, plus she will have around $25,000 to $30,000 in student loans when she graduates." It was an easy call for me to offer LRAP to this family. After I introduced the idea, the Ardeo team explained all of the specific details to the family. Once Samantha signed her LRAP Award letter, she deposited.

Halfway through her academic career, she has already spent time with a number of our writing and publishing alumni and continues to thrive in her creative writing focused English curriculum. Every party wins in this agreement. The family was able to invest in the Illinois Wesleyan education, knowing there were secured guarantees as Samantha launches into the world of professional writing. Samantha can pursue writing with a little less pressure while balancing a full-time job after graduation. Illinois Wesleyan gains a great, mission-fit student who will make the most of her experience.

> **They asked him, "Joseph, how are you going to pay your student loans during the two years you are in the Peace Corps?**

Here's another example of how LRAP affected a student outcome. Joseph heard about Illinois Wesleyan's meaningful connection to the Peace Corps. In fact, one of the Admissions Officers at IWU spent two years in Panama with the Peace Corps and spoke highly of the preparation and connection available at Illinois Wesleyan. Joseph told me, "From everything I have read and heard about the Peace Corps and the education at IWU, I know I am going to be able to make an impact quickly and meaningfully. Everyone that I have talked to who lived the Peace Corps experience speaks of the relationships, critical thinking, problem-solving skills and purpose that follows them every day of their life." There was only one thing that stood in the way of Joseph's decision—his parents. They asked him, "Joseph, how are you going to pay your student loans during the two years that you are in the Peace Corps?" While Joseph struggled to respond, I was able to talk about LRAP with his family. Once again, LRAP provided an excellent fit for the student, the family and Illinois Wesleyan.

Meet Andre. I knew Andre was going to take the campus by storm the minute I met him. He had big plans. Andre would be the first person in his family with the opportunity to attend college. And after just a few minutes of conversation, I knew that if I could be part of his story, it would be the best thing I did all year. And if Illinois Wesleyan could be part of his story, it would be transformational. When he was packaged, we matched Andre with every possible scholarship and grant internally and externally, but loans would still have to be part of the financial aid proposal. I do not doubt that public schools gave him scholarships and grant proposals that were all-encompassing, perhaps with no loans at all. But Andre knew, his mom knew and I knew that he would not have the same experience, in a crowded classroom on a massive campus, that he would at Illinois Wesleyan. Andre and his family were a bit afraid of the loans and what those payments might be four or five years from matriculation. Being able to say: "Andre, what if I told you we could guarantee that even if you do not have the quick start in your career that all of us think you will, we could make sure your loan repayments are reimbursed? Would that help put your mind at ease?" Being able to hear the words: "Yes! Yes, that would make a huge difference," from Andre and his family is precisely the reason why Illinois Wesleyan participates in the LRAP program.

> "Without the great work of your admissions team, without your caring faculty and LRAP, I would not be able to make this dream come to fruition."

Each year during our partnership with LRAP, almost 100% of the depositing students share this with me: "Without the great work of your Admissions team, without your caring faculty and LRAP, I would not be able to make this dream come to fruition."

For a small investment per student per year, students are now choosing IWU who would have never been able to make it work without this additional assurance. Our data tells us that our graduates will not have to use the extra protection LRAP affords, but now more than ever, the unknowns of the labor landscape make this peace of mind more and more valuable. In calculating the net-tuition revenue from the students who have shared with me they would otherwise not have been able to choose Illinois Wesleyan University, the total in three years is over $1.2 million. For an institution that knows return on investment well, that is as good as it gets!

With approximately 1,700 total undergraduates at Illinois Wesleyan, LRAP offers another, less obvious benefit. It allows our team to connect with many students personally as we work through the process together. I can walk through the dining commons during the week and see several students I remember talking to in an admissions interview, college fair, open house or last-minute April visit. Many of the conversations about LRAP allow me to get to know the students and families deeper. I hear the hesitation in their voices, but it is never as loud as the desire and dream of a student who wants to make IWU their home.

In the three years since I joined Illinois Wesleyan and we chose to add LRAP to our toolbox, IWU has experienced its first total enrollment increase in more than 10 years as well as two of our most diverse incoming classes.

All of our counselors work with a large number of admitted students each recruitment cycle. We set the pace for the personal connections the students will enjoy over the next four years. The opportunity to ask a student, even two years after you've met, "Are you working on that first novel?" or "Are you still excited about the Peace Corps?" To see the light in their eyes, the realization of a meaningful connection and knowing someone is listening is when I feel so good about our work. I know there are times when the educational investment is a stretch for a family. Still, I am confident about the experience and opportunities each student will have at Illinois Wesleyan.

In the three years since I joined Illinois Wesleyan and we chose to add LRAP to our toolbox, IWU has experienced its first total enrollment increase in more than 10 years as well as two of our most diverse incoming classes. With the incoming class of 2018, LRAP helped us add 14 racially and socioeconomically diverse students, filling every first-year spot on campus. In 2019, we used LRAP in the same way to see similar success. In 2020, even amid a pandemic, we have filled every new student spot on campus—our new student increase was 9%. We were one of the few schools in the

Midwest, perhaps even the country, to have new-student growth.

As the COVID-19 pandemic has disproportionately impacted our diverse communities nationally, we have been able to use LRAP to give families peace about the decision to make Illinois Wesleyan University their home. If LRAP can help the institution live out its mission in better ways to a broader audience, I am thrilled to sing and share its praise!

CHAPTER 7

THE BEST YIELD TOOL I EVER USED

MATT OSBORNE
SPRING ARBOR UNIVERSITY

W e've all heard the analogy of the frog in the kettle of boiling water. Well, that frog was nearly me. I was in my 16th year serving as a Vice President of Enrollment at my second institution. We had made good strides in the first six years at Spring Arbor University, growing the traditional undergraduate enrollment from just over 1,000 students to over 1,600. However, every year my team worked harder to achieve our goals since our yield rates kept dropping. Nothing precipitous, but it was a steady decline. There were too many good to great-fit students who walked away due to affordability concerns. They faced the challenges of borrowing funds for a career that would earn a modest salary. Frankly, I was growing concerned and frustrated. I really didn't want to be the frog in the kettle.

During that year, Peter Samuelson, a former student employee of mine, from a much earlier point in my career, approached me with an idea. I say an idea because he hadn't yet found a college that

ABOUT THE AUTHOR: Matt Osborne is the Senior Vice President of Client Service at Ardeo Education Solutions. He is the former Vice President of Enrollment at Spring Arbor University, where he helped increase their main campus undergraduate enrollment by over 60% with Ardeo's LRAPs. Matt earned a bachelor's from Greenville University and a master's from Southern Illinois University at Edwardsville.

was willing to be a pioneer. The idea, a Loan Repayment Assistance Program (LRAP), sounded intriguing. It had the potential to address the fear of student loan debt that so many families often expressed as they walked away. As my friend and Ardeo colleague, Roger Kieffer, would later come to say, "It just made sense." I approached my CFO, and together we decided to pilot LRAP. On April 14, 2008, we signed an agreement and became the first client of the LRAP Association (now Ardeo Education Solutions).

> On April 14, 2008, we signed an agreement and became the first client of the LRAP Association (now Ardeo Education Solutions).

My agreement with the CFO stated that we wouldn't exceed 10 students in that first year. After all, an LRAP is a significant promise, with a possible long tail for the number of years that a graduate might need support. The LRAP Association was a new company. What if they didn't make it, and we at the college would need to take on the responsibility of assisting the graduates? As their first client, it seemed wise to start small.

I began my utilization by asking my admissions representatives to nominate students they believed were fearful of student loans. It was a one-off, selective process. We ended up signing and enrolling two to three students in this way. Given that it was already mid-April, I also had my reps review every accepted student with a financial aid package who hadn't deposited. These students were ranked on their likelihood to enroll. Those who were less likely we called fence-sitters; they were sent a letter about LRAP. The letter was mailed to their parents. Even then, I realized parents would be the primary audience for understanding and appreciating the LRAP promise.

The letter shared the basics about LRAP and invited parents to call me with questions or learn more about this new program. It indicated there were a limited number of LRAP slots available. One of the parents I heard from shared that his daughter had just canceled her application with us and had already made plans to attend the local community college. We obviously had a snapshot in time issue between pulling the data and receiving his daughter's cancellation. He asked several questions, primarily centered around the idea that an LRAP wouldn't cost him or his daughter anything. I think he used these two clichés at least once: "There's no such thing as a free lunch." "What's the catch?" Having addressed his questions, he asked if he could still have a week to consider this opportunity because he saw it as a game-changer. I assured him that he could have the week which was the amount of time the letter had indicated. Unfortunately, at the end of that week, he called back to apologize. He shared that his daughter was just too far down the road in her commitment to the community college. She had already submitted her housing deposit, received her room assignment and talked to her roommate. This was another lesson learned in understanding that an LRAP isn't a silver bullet, and the timing of offers is essential. Providing hope to a family while Spring Arbor was still on their shortlist proved to be critical.

> **Even then, I realized parents would be the primary audience for understanding and appreciating the LRAP promise.**

By the end of the week, I had more than enough desirable LRAP candidates—19 students for the seven remaining slots. Having reviewed these students alongside their majors and financial aid packages, I made calls to the parents. In three cases, the parents realized their son or daughter would likely make more money than the upper-income threshold, yet they thanked me for the consideration, and their student still enrolled. I sensed the added attention and conversation helped them appreciate their students' likely higher starting salary and addressed their concerns over borrowing, which allowed them to support enrollment.

I was still faced with deciding how to move forward with the eight remaining worthy families because I only had seven slots left. Each had expressed they would need an LRAP to enroll. I brought the final three cases for two remaining slots back to my CFO. I decided to put him in the position of a King Solomon role. Once we reviewed the net revenue represented by each student, he agreed that moving from 10 total slots to 11 made perfect sense. The ROI of the additional net revenue entirely justified the additional investment of the LRAP fee.

I found it interesting that there was much more diversity in the profile in this first small group of 11 students than I had expected. My top majors at SAU included teacher education, psychology, business, ministry and art. In fact, we had one of the most extensive art programs of any private college in the state. I had guessed that I would have five or more art students in the 10 original slots. While I did end up with two art majors and one communications major, I also had an actuarial studies major and a chemistry major. In terms of loan borrowing behavior, I had assumed a majority of students would borrow well above the federal student loan minimum of $5,500. While I did end up with one student who had a total loan portfolio of $17,000, the simple majority of the students were only utilizing the $5,500 of federal student loans. In short, the one true common denominator among these students was their family's fear of loans and an LRAP's ability to provide peace of mind if they had to borrow and enroll.

> **The one true common denominator among these students was their family's fear of loans and an LRAP's ability to provide peace of mind if they had to borrow and enroll.**

Perhaps as a sidebar, I should mention that in my years now working at Ardeo, I'm often asked whether utilizing an LRAP will encourage undue borrowing. Both my first-year cohort above and our studies would indicate that isn't the case. An increase in the percentage of the class borrowing should be expected since a college will now enroll students who previously wouldn't have borrowed due to fear of loans. Similarly, a relative increase in borrowing can be expected as a function of continued tuition and/or room and board increases. An LRAP will allow a family to deem it worthwhile to borrow and cover those additional costs rather than not enroll or dropout (if a current student).

The following year I had an agreement with the CFO to increase the number of new LRAP students to 25. He did not want us to offer LRAP to transfers because, at that time, the fee was higher for that population than for first-year students. (This is no longer the case.) My transfer counselor and I didn't quite see it that way. Instead, we made some offers to transfers. We justified it by covering the differential between the freshman fee and the transfer fee by lowering all the institutional grants by $50 to transfers. Dropping the institutional grant by $50 wouldn't change any enrollment decisions but providing an LRAP to a handful certainly would. We were correct on both counts, and after explaining the rationale to the CFO, he agreed that it was a good move. This was another lesson learned. One way to account for LRAP fees is to arbitrage the fees via your institutional aid budget.

> I found it interesting that there was much more diversity in the profile in this first small group of 11 students than I had expected.

We continued to utilize LRAP in these ways over the ensuing three years, but in the third year, the wheels totally came off, and our overall new freshman enrollment plummeted from a class of 405 to 313. Needless to say, there was a great deal of pain associated with this reality. Staff were laid off. Faculty had to take on an additional course within their load. Fringe benefits were reduced. It wasn't pleasant. On a personal level, I was concerned about my job security for the first time in my career. The President even hired a firm to conduct an audit of our admissions office. Fortunately, I had several good years in the bank to also see the President approve a research study on the possibility of a tuition reset. We believed our low new student enrollment was an indication of having exceeded our market's price point. Over 30% of my class was typically first-generation students, and 40% to 50% were Pell-eligible. Having reviewed a number of proposals, we selected Stamats to conduct the research.

Stamats surveyed the parents of high school seniors in our funnel immediately after Labor Day of their senior year. Within the standard questions related to our pricing reset, we also integrated a question about LRAP. The basic concept was to ask any parents selecting our competitors rather than SAU whether their decision would change if SAU provided a loan repayment assistance program. This was asked after they read a three-sentence description of an LRAP. Stamats came back with their findings. We could pursue a pricing reset, which they believed would yield a 3% increase in enrollment beyond the norm. But they indicated that we'd need to spend over $600,000 in additional marketing to effectively message and announce the reset. Their findings on the parents' response to an LRAP were more dramatic and positive. They believed that by marketing an LRAP broadly, we would grow the class from 313 to 360! In addition, they didn't see the need for significantly increasing the marketing budget to promote the LRAP since we could integrate LRAP messaging within our regular efforts.

> **They believed that by marketing an LRAP broadly, we would grow the class from 313 to 360!**

SAU's cabinet met with Peter Samuelson to review the cost/benefit analysis. The data indicated that of the projected increase of 47 students, we would need the additional revenue from 22 students to cover the expected cost of the fees for all of the borrowers within the class. This approach—covering the cost of the fees entirely from the growth—echoed my concern and doubts regarding the possible use of lowering institutional grants. Additionally, since the fees were per student borrower, this wasn't a typical risk analysis where the initiative's success or failure would entirely hinge on gaining at least 22 additional students for two reasons. First, for each student less than the projected 360, there would be a corresponding drop in the fees. Therefore, an incremental decrease in the number of additional students is needed to breakeven. Second, even in the event of a more dramatic misstep, the impact of enrolling each student below the breakeven number would result in simply losing the average net revenue of a student. Based on that analysis and the strength of the Stamats' research results, the decision was made to move forward.

At the moment of decision, I was both energized and petrified. Why? I was energized because broadly marketing an LRAP would provide me with a key-value proposition to address a fundamental concern for many families in my market. I was petrified because the decision was made in early November. This is, of course, late in a recruitment cycle for rolling out a campaign if you wish to impact the top of your funnel. It was well after all of my collateral had been printed, and after most of the fall travel season when I could have otherwise had my team share the news with students and parents and high school counselors—after the bulk of my outside sourced senior search and application campaigns. It was late. You can certainly understand why I was nervous.

I still remember one of my Admissions Reps returning to the office after visiting a high school. Near the end of her conversation with the counselor, she was asked if she had a few more minutes. She did, and the counselor walked her down the hall to a senior English class and asked the teacher to give my rep a few minutes to share information about our LRAP with the class. She had "never heard of anything like it," and "she wanted these college-bound students to hear about it." My rep had never had such a whole-hearted response from a counselor, at least not one that wasn't an alum of SAU. She was still smiling ear-to-ear when she got back to the office, and after she shared the story, so was I.

She had "never heard of anything like it," and "she wanted these college-bound students to hear about it."

I've discovered that type of response to LRAP isn't uncommon. Another one of Ardeo's partners shared that while traveling the state of Washington providing high school counselors updates by region across the state (all the colleges in the state are invited to caravan across the state to do so), their admissions counselor shared information about their LRAP. While the typical announcements are about new academic programs or new facilities, the LRAP announcement drew applause and a standing ovation from some. This product is pretty straightforward. An LRAP can persuade influencers and has the potential power to shift them from gatekeeper to promoter.

Less than a week after the decision was made to offer LRAPs to all SAU incoming freshmen, and before we had any printed materials to share, we had an overnight campus visit event with about 75 students and parents in attendance. On the opening evening, we always had separate programming for the parents, including a financial aid session. While we didn't have our printed mailing insert ready to hand out yet, Ardeo had provided us with some of what they called candy grams. This is a sweet reminder of what an LRAP does. Utilizing three mini candy bars—a 100 Grand, a Payday and a roll of Lifesavers—the card included in the packet contains this statement: "If you are worried that your college will cost you 100 Grand and that you will graduate to a small Payday, then an LRAP is your Lifesaver."

> "If you are worried that your college will cost you 100 Grand and that you will graduate to a small Payday, then an LRAP is your Lifesaver."

When the LRAP slides were projected on the screen, there was an audible response… some gasps were heard. Then the candy grams were handed out, and there were some chuckles. After the session, a mother approached me. She held up the candy gram and said that it was "pretty cheesy," but she'd likely never forget it. It was a small thing but another reassurance that we had made the right decision to market our LRAP broadly.

After that decision, I immediately asked my marketing colleagues to create a mailing insert. It wasn't much, but my collateral budget was already spent. The piece's theme was, "You are not a loan." This would play on the idea that we would partner with the family—they wouldn't be alone when it came to the question of repayment of educational loans. We included this insert in all mailings from the admissions and financial aid offices. While an LRAP was obviously not our exclusive value proposition, we saw it as an enabling proposition—one which would provide the tipping point for a family who wanted their student to attend.

The marketing department also attempted to gain some attention in the media but to no avail. For whatever reason, it just didn't catch the media's attention. It may have had something to do with the timing, as it was immediately following a presidential election. Interestingly, an additional effort was made to gain media attention in February, this time utilizing a PR firm's services. A local TV station covered us by coming to campus and interviewing our President. From that small beginning, the AP picked it up, and we were the buzz. Interviews were conducted on radio stations in Chicago and newspapers in Los Angeles. Pundits weighed in on radio, TV and print. On the Friday afternoon of that week, our website crashed due to all the traffic. I know the initial TV interview was the genesis of all that followed. In that reporter's initial story published online, she incorrectly captured the LRAP fee amount by adding a zero. This made our fee look so large that it likely drove some of the discussions within the media.

The three freedoms provided by LRAP:

- **Freedom to attend the college they want**
- **Freedom to study what they want**
- **Freedom to pursue the career they want**

Yet despite our efforts and even with the media response, we must have been too late in the cycle to influence the top of the funnel. Our application and accepted numbers were within one percentage point of the previous year. The year with the dismal results. What changed was yield! Stamats research was validated. Between my team's hard work and the promise of LRAP, we didn't just increase the enrollment from 313 to 360 as Stamats had predicted; we instead enrolled 370 freshmen that fall.

I saw the validation of LRAP in providing access to students and what I refer to as the three freedoms provided by an LRAP:

- Freedom to attend the college they want
- Freedom to study what they want
- Freedom to pursue the career they want

I knew this was a game-changer for families and enrollment professionals, and it also became a game-changer for me. I determined I could pursue my professional calling by joining the Ardeo team. The day that the entering class of 2013, the first full class to benefit from LRAPs, moved on to campus at SAU was my last day as their Vice President for Enrollment.

The following day I began my tenure at Ardeo, where it has been a joy to share my story with other enrollment professionals. It has been rewarding to see others discover the power of LRAP in changing enrollment decisions and changing lives. Weekly, I review the testimonial responses of students who have just signed their LRAP Award. They share their family's stories of their finances and their angst regarding their possibilities of attending their first-choice college. They testify to the relief the LRAP safety-net has provided to them and their parents.

It's incredibly gratifying to play a role in the lives of so many students. These future graduates—who have been changed by their education—will go on to make significant contributions to society.

> It's incredibly gratifying to play a role in the lives of so many students. These future graduates—who have been changed by their education—will go on to make significant contributions to society.

Similarly, it has given me great pleasure to have worked with nearly 70 colleges as they've launched and utilized our LRAP to help them achieve various aspects of their enrollment and revenue goals. The enrollment profession isn't an easy one and with the coming demographic shifts will only become more difficult, so providing such an effective and efficient tool to my colleagues in the trenches has been very gratifying. I love having the opportunity to fulfill my calling in this way.

CHAPTER 8

SUPPORTING THE ALMA FAMILY

AMANDA ZIELINSKI SLENSKI
ALMA COLEGE

A t Alma College, we tailor all we do to the needs, goals and aspirations of our individual students; our use of Ardeo's Loan Repayment Assistance Program (LRAP) is an excellent example. Alma College is a private liberal arts college with approximately 1,450 students located in the heart of Michigan's Lower Peninsula. The college has a strong Scottish heritage, a close-knit and caring campus community, a plaid sense of style and a love for the sound of bagpipes drifting through the air.

Founded in 1886, the College has remained intentionally small while maintaining a growth mindset and ensuring we offer personalized education to aspiring students who find their home at Alma. We are mission-driven preparing graduates who think critically, serve generously, lead purposefully and live responsibly as stewards of the world, bequeathing these qualities to future generations.

With over 95% of our graduates employed or enrolled in

ABOUT THE AUTHOR: Amanda Zielinski Slenski serves as the Vice President for Admissions and Special Assistant to the President at Alma College (MI). She is passionate about supporting students and families through the college search process and doing her part to ensure accessibility and affordability in higher education. Amanda earned a bachelor's degree from Alma College and a master's degree from Miami University (OH).

graduate school within the first six months after graduation, we know an Alma education prepares students well for their next step, whether that is a job or graduate school. Our graduates leave Alma College with a greater understanding of the world and their place in it, ready to pursue passions, serve their communities and succeed as professionals.

We are a community of scholars that comes together to support one another and works to ensure the success of our students. An Alma education is a worthy investment that will continue to pay dividends for years to come. Our student population has historically included a large percentage of students with a high level of financial need, as determined by the Free Application for Federal Student Aid (FAFSA) and first-generation college students. We look at an Alma education as a shared investment, and we are strongly committed to access and affordability for our students. We help ensure they have financial support through merit and interest-based scholarships and need-based financial aid. Over the last 10 years, we have seen a dramatic increase in the number of students and families who have come to us to express their interest in Alma; however, even with our generous support, they have concerns about out-of-pocket costs.

> **Alma's admissions and financial aid staff need to have resources available to meet the concerns expressed by students and their families.**

Alma draws the vast majority of our students from our home state. Therefore, many students looking at Alma College are also considering large, regional universities and state schools. As a state with a declining high school student population and an abundance of high-quality higher education institutions, the market competition is fierce, especially for small, private, tuition-driven institutions. In response to this competition and due to a statewide commitment to post-secondary degree attainment, high discount and free college options are commonplace.

Michigan has witnessed an influx of "promise zones" since the start of the Kalamazoo Promise in 2009, which was the country's first community-based universal scholarship program. Promise programs commit to covering some or all of the tuition for students from communities across the state. Many of these promise scholarships require students stay within their community to utilize the benefit, which makes recruiting students from those areas more challenging. We have partnered with promise programs whenever possible. We are proud to also offer the Kalamazoo and Detroit promise programs on our campus, along with an institutional program that supports up to 10 local students a year to attend tuition-free. Still, we have found that since we've put the programs in place, it has been challenging to recruit students from these geographic areas. This additional layer to our competitive landscape necessitates that we take a comprehensive and strategic approach to our students' financial support.

> **Concerns from families continue to surge due to the news media's prevalent stories about student loan debt rising across the country.**

Alma's admissions and financial aid staff need to have resources available to meet the concerns expressed by students and their families. A liberal arts college experience, like at Alma College, has great value attached to it, but it is not inexpensive for students. We believe small classes with tenured faculty who hold terminal degrees is worth the additional expense, but it costs more to deliver that experience to students. Many families need to finance some portion of their student's Alma education through federal and/or private loan programs, even with generous financial aid. Concerns about taking out student loans and students' ability to make payments on those loans is a regular topic of conversation during the college search and selection process.

Concerns from families continue to surge due to the news media's prevalent stories about student loan debt rising across the country. Families are equally concerned their students may be unable to find stable employment upon graduation. We have also noticed an increase in the number of parents who are still paying on their own student loans from their undergraduate or graduate education as their child looks to enter college. This makes it difficult for parents, in this situation, to contribute as much as they would like to their child's education. Additional pressure weighs on the students to ensure they can begin making their loan payments immediately following their degree. In 2011, Alma College began to look for a new way to respond to these concerns felt by students and families to better respond to their apprehensions.

This is where LRAP came in. We heard about LRAP through a peer institution that began offering it to their entire incoming class. It sparked curiosity about how we might be able to effectively utilize this program for our institution as well. I still remember the first time I heard of LRAP and learned that we would be bringing it to Alma. I was an Admissions Representative at the time, making a salary below the threshold for LRAP support and still paying on my student loans from my own time at Alma (proud Scot – Class of 2007). I saw how much I would have benefitted from the program. Although it was too late for me, I instantly thought of all of the students we could help. I was immediately impressed by the program and the potential for life-changing support it could provide to our students.

I was immediately impressed by the program and the potential for life-changing support it could provide to our students.

At that time, a full offering to a large group of incoming students did not seem to fit us. However, we saw considerable promise in the program and knew it would greatly benefit some of our students. We needed to find an approach suited to our students and our consultative recruitment efforts. We determined we would fund a certain number of spots for incoming students and identify the program's best fit.

When we hear concerns about student loan debt, about co-signing on a private loan for a student, about taking out a Parent PLUS loan or a private loan, we have a solution. As we sit with families and hear about a student's dream to go into a field that does not traditionally lead to a high starting salary, and we see the concern on a parent's face, we have a solution. When we have students who want to go into service-based fields, which is a core tenet of our mission, we have a solution. When students are unsure of what they want to study and are concerned about the future, but they know Alma is the right fit for them, we have a solution.

LRAP has become that solution for us.

We believe in the value of an Alma education and share that value proposition with the students and families considering Alma. We know there will always be a less expensive option for students, so our value proposition is critical to share with prospective students. LRAP is part of reinforcing that benefit. Our message to students is this: "We believe so fully that you will be successful after Alma that we will commit to offering you LRAP to provide additional security for your future." We often talk about the "tools in our toolbox" to assist families. These tools include donor-based scholarships, an institutional loan program, a guaranteed job program, discretionary aid and, of course, LRAP.

> Our message to students is this: "We believe so fully that you will be successful after Alma that we will commit to offering you LRAP to provide additional security for your future."

These students are more than just a name or a number to us. From the moment we first encounter them in the admissions process, we engage in intentional and meaningful consultative recruitment. In doing so, we know these students, their families and their stories. We know which students are financing college on their own, or the ones who want to be dancers or musicians. We know whose families are worried about their ability to make ends meet after graduation. We know the students who are undecided about what they want to do in the future—and we love it—but their parents, not always as much. We know the dreamers and the doers, the ones bound for medical school or the Peace Corps. We know the independent students and the single parents. We know those who are worried about the day their first bill will come, and the ones who have been saving for college for decades. We know the ones who are excited about this next step and their future and the ones who are concerned about what is to come and scared of the unknown. We welcome them all and work with them to make Alma College an affordable reality.

There is not an algorithm or data pull that can replicate what we do at Alma with LRAP. We match LRAP with students based on a student's needs, intended career path, overall aid package, family support, potential loans and so much more. It is an art more than a science, and we see every day its impact on families. The stories become part of the narrative of Alma College and the student experience. Some students are like Jared, who shared with us how much the program gives him security to pursue his education and his career; or Hannah, who was provided with confidence to make the financial commitment to attend Alma; or Michael, who had a fear of taking out student loans, and it was LRAP that eased those fears.

> There is not an algorithm or data pull that can replicate what we do at Alma with LRAP.

The student experiences we hear about year after year reiterate the importance of our partnership with Ardeo. LRAP has made an Alma College education possible for these individuals who will contribute to our campus community and learn and grow during their time here and beyond. The students above chose Alma, and they are successful. They make a significant impact on our campus and our community, and they will continue to make a lasting impact on the communities they engage with long into the future. The support that LRAP provides and the support students receive during their time at Alma quite literally changes their lives.

These students will become educators, volunteers, counselors, artists and so much more.

LRAP provides a safety-net for students to chase their dreams.

We offer an average of 23 LRAP spots per year through individual student outreach, and on average, 86% of those students ultimately enroll. This number varies based on the incoming class's needs and has been as low as eight offers with all eight students enrolling and as high as 46 offers with 29 students enrolling. For many years, we looked at the outgoing number of students and matched our offers to incoming students. However, we learned over time that the needs of each incoming class can vary greatly. One year, the number of undecided students spiked. Fittingly, we utilized more

LRAP spots that year because more concerns were heard from those families about the job prospects for their students who had not yet determined a career path. Another year, a large percentage of the incoming class planned to enter health fields like nursing and medicine—not ideal students for the program since they tend to be high-paying career fields even in entry-level positions.

Rather than trying to hit a specific number, we began to look for specific needs, and this student-centered approach has proven successful. The Admissions team is encouraged to recommend students who would be a good fit for the program and secure them a spot. When we offer a spot in the LRAP program to a student, we want to ensure that they intend to borrow federal or private loans to fund their education. We address concerns about taking on student loan debt to finance an Alma education if the student plans to go into a field that typically does not have high-income entry-level positions available. We also specifically utilize LRAP to support further students with a high financial need and independent students who we look to support in any way possible to make an Alma education a reality.

We have used LRAP since 2011, because we can see its direct impact on our incoming class enrollment and the retention of students.

For us, we have found that offering the program to students individually based on their needs is even more impactful than broad offers because the families feel heard and understood. Their concerns are validated, and we can offer a real, tangible solution.

Over the years, we have tried other means of offering LRAP, such as stale funnel offers and broad appeals to students who have expressed an interest in Alma College. None has had the same impact on our new student enrollment as the individual offers. We will continue to explore new and innovative ways to utilize the program, but our work's core will remain the targeted outreach and personalized matching with the students we know are the best fit.

We have used LRAP since 2011, because we can see its direct impact on our incoming class enrollment and the retention of students.

LRAP is one of the tools we have utilized to maintain our strong overall enrollment during a time with increased competition, a declining high school population, external pressure and higher education challenges. Our tailored approach to identifying "best-fit students" for the program enables us to maximize its impact.

Through LRAP, we link students who are also mission-driven and connect with our college and the Alma experience to the resources they need to make an Alma education a reality. As a college committed to service, we can also specifically support students going into fields that do not traditionally provide high wages but serve communities and make a huge impact, like education.

> **Ardeo is authentic and transparent. The staff values partnership and commitment, and they provide a product that puts students first. The trust and commitment from both sides are continuously apparent.**

The college's partnership with the Ardeo team is also unlike any other vendor relationship we have. Alma has been an Ardeo client for almost a decade—a relationship that has spanned multiple Vice Presidents, Chief Financial Officers and Directors of Admissions. There is one simple reason why that is the case: we see great value in our work together at every level. Ardeo is authentic and transparent. The staff values partnership and commitment, and they provide a product that puts students first. The trust and commitment from both sides are continuously apparent.

We feel as though the Ardeo staff is a true extension of our team. They generate ideas to help us when we do not see the numbers we hope to see. They celebrate with us when a student commits to the college. They check in during trying times, and they take time to work with students and families every step of the way. I am reminded weekly of the time, attention and care they put into everything they do. Ardeo continues to exceed my expectations. They, too, have become a part of the Alma family.

Our work with Ardeo is woven into the work we do to make an Alma education affordable and accessible to students. As the home of the Scots, located in Scotland, USA, our college tartan is a meaningful part of an Alma experience and symbolizes our most cherished values. Tartan fabric is created by weaving threads of different colors to create a beautiful and elaborate pattern. They are woven tightly together for strength, and each tiny thread is needed to complete the final, highly valuable cloth. We look at the Alma College community in the same way, and the Ardeo staff and LRAP program have become a thread within our tartan. They are a piece of the greater whole that is at the core of an Alma College experience and the support network for our students.

Ardeo continues to exceed my expectations. They, too, have become a part of the Alma family.

We have a cherished tradition on our campus. Each year, we host an opening convocation that serves as a bookend to a student's commencement four years later. It has all the same pomp and circumstance—the speeches, the regalia, the bagpipes. During the event, the incoming class is presented to the faculty. All of their outstanding accomplishments are shared. The students sign a Book of Gathering, a time-honored tradition passed along for generations.

The text on the pages reads:

Alma College - A Book of Gathering

We come together to form an academic community, one in which we will learn to think critically, serve generously, lead purposefully, and live responsibly as stewards of the world we bequeath to future generations. With thanks to our families, teachers, and friends who helped us get here, we are ready to engage with our Alma College professors and classmates. We are ready for the challenge, ready to shape and be shaped by the Alma College community.

The book is then presented to the provost and faculty colleagues to symbolize the students' movement into the Alma community, where they will benefit from the guidance and direction of the community of scholars and friends. The book is kept for them during their time at Alma, and it returns at their graduation. The pages are then passed on to our Alumni Association as they officially become Alma College alumni and enter the next chapter of their relationship with the college.

> **We look at our work with LRAP as the next chapter for some of these students.**

We look at our work with LRAP as the next chapter for some of these students. We do all that we can to prepare them for wonderful and lucrative lives and careers. If that is not their intended path, then the students with LRAP have additional support to help them grow. They always have the Alma family to support them throughout their lives. During a time of such great uncertainty, LRAP, and an Alma College education, can provide students with the support they need to embark into a world changed forever.

CHAPTER 9

OPPORTUNITY, WHERE'S THE DOWNSIDE?

DAVE VOSKUIL
EMORY & HENRY COLLEGE

Entering my second year as Vice President of Enrollment Management at Emory & Henry College (E&H), I was in the process of completing my professional career as an "admission guy," committing to a contract for three recruitment cycles to stabilize and grow enrollment. With more than 40 years in the enrollment profession, I joined the small, liberal arts, religiously affiliated college located just north of the Virginia-Tennessee border. I settled in the farmlands of Emory, Virginia, looking forward to both the challenges and opportunities an institution like Emory & Henry provides.

Nestled in the foothills of the Appalachian Mountains on I-81, E&H is your typical, small private college, with a myriad of colleges similar in profile and size located throughout the state. Like most, E&H depended on tuition dollars to sustain the long tradition of a quality, personalized, Christian education. Many higher

---

ABOUT THE AUTHOR: Dave Voskuil is the former Vice President for Enrollment Management at Emory & Henry College. He has more than 40 years of higher education experience in admission and financial aid. He has proven success in the private college and university sector, serving seven institutions as Chief Enrollment Officer and acting as a Consultant to 12 private, liberal arts colleges.

education leaders and educators I've met over the course of my career believe whole-heartedly that their institution far out strides the competition, but nobody knows it because we need a more comprehensive admissions plan. Loving the place at which you work, perhaps your alma mater, is wonderful. Every organization needs people who believe in it. Unfortunately, I have often found that love can be blinding.

E&H faces stiff competition. There are 19 four-year private colleges in Virginia alone.

E&H faces stiff competition. There are 19 four-year private colleges in Virginia alone. Within four hours of E&H, there are six other schools lined up the I-81 corridor on the way to Washington, DC—all with similar missions and messaging.

I knew I needed outside strategies to support my plan to foster new student growth with cost-efficient initiatives due to budget constraints.

We began with some initial strategies in an attempt to turn the tide:

- **Direct Mail Campaign** – We added more names and enhanced the communications plan. We partnered with a firm to develop printed marketing pieces to ensure timely contact.

  Results: Increased applications by 18%. However, applications aren't guaranteed enrollments.

- **New Website** – We restructured staff for website development, reassigning from the public relations department to the enrollment management department. We began heightened tracking of inquiry hits and started the redesign of the website while also focusing on navigation ease and efficiency.

  Results: Increased quality of applications received.

- **Awarding of Aid** – We eased the road to admission and the awarding of aid. We broke down barriers to complete the application for review and the implementation of a holistic approach to admission and awarding of aid. There was less emphasis on standardized testing results.

  Results: Increased admitted students.

- **Marketing Plan Targeting Transfer Students** – We developed a marketing plan and award program specific to the transfer market. We broke down some past norms regarding the transfer of credits, with compelling articulation agreements.

  Results: Increased new transfer student enrollment both in fall and spring semesters. We updated transfer articulations with local community colleges that included scholarship commitments to qualified admits.

  > **We began with some initial strategies in an attempt to turn the tide.**

- **Appeals Process for Financial Aid** – We understood the student/family's desire to negotiate the financial aid award. We implemented an "appeals process" to address this and compete with our competitors.

  Results: Saved 10 deposits in the initial year.

- **Proactive Merit Financial Aid Program** – We implemented early estimates and payment options supporting the investment we were making with families.

  Results: Increased deposits received before May 1.

Some of these strategies needed approval from the internal cabinet to be implemented as policy while some tactics were implemented around the internal departments, committees, etc., but they did little to improve the perception of the product we were selling. And, in my opinion, an investment in the brand and working with a marketing firm was not the answer. Therefore, my awareness of any opportunity to enhance the product with a meaningful benefit was an important addition to the tactics we implemented to clear the way for the students to follow their passions. These strategies and programs, implemented to stabilize enrollment and increase new student numbers, were more foundational. I believe they aided in the enrollment growth turnaround I was seeking. Knowing additional help was needed, I was open to an opportunity with a vendor who would set us apart from our competitors.

The enrollment profession is flooded with higher education vendors who promise a solution to whatever your problem is.

You need more new freshmen? We have a solution.

More transfers? No problem.

Need to leverage your financial aid effectively? We'll increase revenues for sure.

Retention an issue for your campus? We'll bring in the team to solve it.

Need a new brand? We will bring a suitcase full, one which will surely distinguish you from your competition and bring your campus together as one.

> **At E&H, developing a "culture" of enrollment management on the campus was important to me.**

You're off to the races. As a VP, you listen, read and review the pitch. You meet representatives at conferences or through your colleagues. At E&H, developing a "culture" of enrollment management on the campus was important to me. I felt this foundation, or at least the building of this enrollment foundation, was crucial when looking for a vendor who sells the solution and has the so-called "silver bullet." With this understanding, I began looking for collaboration with a vendor, a partner, who would support this same culture of enrollment management on a campus that needed stability. Cue Ardeo.

During my career, I worked with an enrollment professional and former CEO of Target Market. I utilized both his services and his insights in enrollment development which supported my success as an enrollment professional. So, when he contacted me about this new firm LRAP Association—now Ardeo Education Solutions—and the program they were pitching, I listened. The LRAP product seemed real and unique. It was also new. I was looking for strategies that enhanced our ability to recruit and retain, in other words, foundational enrollment stability, which ain't rocket science. So, I was teed up to meet Ardeo's Jonathan Shores, who wanted to convince me this was a strategy worth considering.

My approach in determining whether a vendor has something valuable to offer my institution is through conversation, often outside the office. At first, the idea of offering this opportunity to all freshmen at a fee for those enrolling was interesting and noble, but was it affordable? I had other ideas for using the product. Jonathan listened as we considered alternative strategies to utilize this product. Thankfully, I didn't get five email follow-ups with the word "solutions." I received alternatives and meaningful discussion on Ardeo's options. In addition, we had a meaningful exchange regarding the enrollment profession and challenges colleges like E&H face in the current environment. Yes, social times were also included over a beverage or round of golf—where true ideas often come to fruition.

The key to the LRAP model for me was the investment made directly related to the student, student by student, and not materials, supposed expertise, technology, etc., with the potential to attract more students.

Jonathan became my backboard for bouncing off ideas, questions, justification, strategies and ROI graphs. At institutions like E&H, operating budgets are tight and expenditures, especially in enrollment management, must show a compelling justification with the initial investment providing a tangible return on that investment: enrolling more students. The key to the LRAP model for me was the investment made directly related to the student, student by student, and not materials, supposed expertise, technology, etc., with the potential to attract more students. Additionally, we would be the first and only Virginia college to offer the LRAP benefit. I also liked that E&H only paid when LRAP worked—a student enrolled and borrowed. Plus, in order to benefit from the program, the student would have to graduate from E&H.

Looking at LRAP as an enrollment professional, I realized it would help us achieve basic and essential outcomes we were working toward every day. It would help us attract more students, retain more students and graduate more students. Additionally, it had the capacity to encourage more alumni giving back to the college.

These points were vetted with Jonathan in a variety of conversations as I prepared my internal "pitch" for approval.

One would assume the approval would be a slam dunk, given this strategy would support a successful enrollment outcome. Our enrollment team was excited! Offer LRAP to all freshmen, as an added benefit, and build the cost per student into the budget. With a 30% increase in enrollment, the added cost would be covered with increased net-tuition revenue. But what assurances did we have that new student enrollment would increase 30%? Or 20%? How could we be sure most of those students wouldn't have enrolled anyway without the LRAP benefit? With rising discount rates and a tight operational budget, where would this added budget line be parked? Are there alternatives? The work had just begun.

> **The beauty of the program was the fact that for any payment made to LRAP, the student must be enrolled and graduate for the student to realize the benefit.**

All new "vendor" opportunities awaiting approval at tuition-driven, small colleges with enrollment struggles are institutionally budget-driven. With many divisional heads at the trough for limited dollars to invest in their departmental program/plans, where does the funding go to make the college more attractive?

In the enrollment world, we were competing internally with:

- Capital campaign (advancement) that will need a consultant and marketing funds to kick it off
- Faculty enrichment, development, and sabbatical time to grow new programs
- Deferred maintenance and facility improvements
- Rising salaries and benefits expenses
- Technology infrastructure

We face challenges when we want to fund an enrollment vendor many presidents haven't heard of in their annual meetings. I have used vendors in my 40-year career, but mostly for heightening efficiency in processes where I had a lack of resources or institutional expertise. LRAP was a bit unique in offering a value-added benefit to the students and the institutional brand.

I began the internal PR process necessary to approve a vendor who could uniquely influence our enrollment. Ardeo's initial proposal offered this benefit as a "blanket" to all new incoming freshmen. This "value-added" benefit, used as a selling point for a college that needed to distinguish itself in the competitive private sector, was precisely what I was looking for. But the investment was a hurdle to jump over in running a very tight budget. I needed a second option to the "all incoming freshmen" strategy. This is where significant discussion began with Jonathan and how E&H developed a program that supported our enrollment challenges, stayed within our budget and was also acceptable to the college. These discussions proved how open Ardeo was to working with the college on developing a program. We discussed student segments to which we could offer LRAP including cohorts at risk or under "recruited" over the years as well as to students who were considering leaving the College. We also discussed the majors we wanted to attract.

For years, Counselors often heard the words "I can't afford it" when they followed up with student families after the financial aid award packages were received.

I pushed the discussion with a global enrollment impact. I wanted to consider an Ardeo strategy beyond just new freshmen. Here's what we considered.

- **New Students** - New students considering a major in religion, education or humanities—all of whom are likely to enter the workforce at a low salary.

- **Out-of-State Students** - We have always struggled to attract students from our neighboring states, especially since the state grant does not travel across the border.

  Can we afford to supplement or fund the grant amount with institutional aid and pay for this cohort's Loan Repayment

Assistance Program? (Another good discussion.)

Ardeo once again demonstrated the importance of working with our institution on diverse strategies to support enrollment stability while providing a meaningful benefit for students entering college.

- **New Transfer Market** - Focus on the new transfer market as a cohort to offer to. As an emerging market to help stabilize enrollment overall, I pitched this market to LRAP for consideration.

The "traditional" liberal arts emphasis at institutions I served typically focused on the incoming freshmen who meet the desired profile, attend four years, graduate as a grateful alumni and live life as a "global citizen." But there was growing realization the transfer market did, and does, provide a crucial pipeline of new students who need consideration. LRAP saw this in our discussions and extended its program to include this cohort of students, which was a substantial benefit to E&H.

- **Current Continuing Students** - It's no secret. Many smaller, private colleges struggle to retain students to graduation, especially from enrollment to the third semester. What strategy could Ardeo provide to keep our students enrolled and committed to a degree at our institution? Again, Ardeo went to the drawing board in looking at alternative programming to consider this important segment for any meaningful enrollment management plan. This is now an option Ardeo provides to its clients.

- **Students Seeking More Aid** - During the final five or so years of my professional career, negotiation of the financial aid award became more of the norm rather than the exception when dealing with the parents as true consumers. I became very attentive to the reality of family negation in our profession, realizing there were workshops offered to parents on this process.

As a result, I developed an appeal protocol to address

this reality years before my E&H position and to consider as an alternative to the then-popular policy colleges preferred to implement: "We don't negotiate." I knew this policy would challenge our ability to grow enrollment, and I implemented the appeals process at E&H, incorporating the admission and financial teams in establishing it. I discussed this unique cohort of potential students with Jonathan and Ardeo as a targeted segment for LRAP.

I initiated our first contract with Ardeo using the appeal process strategy. These requests were rising, and LRAP would become a negotiation tool as we formalized the appeal process. This process became personalized and was dependent on each student and family situation. We took into account the family EFC, amount of aid already awarded, location, major, profile and the holistic review by counselor, etc. After review and consultation between the Admission Counselor, Directors of Financial Aid and Admission, and myself, we had three response options: additional institutional aid, job on campus or nothing. With LRAP, we now had a fourth. In almost all cases, we chose to provide LRAP rather than provide more aid (discount) or nothing, knowing this was a benefit to the student while also an investment supporting retention if the student accepted.

> In almost all cases, we chose to provide LRAP rather than provide more aid (discount) or nothing, knowing this was a benefit to the student while also an investment supporting retention if the student accepted.

There were other benefits with the LRAP product. The appeal process had ownership within the Admission Office and the Admission Counselors. For years, Counselors often heard the words "I can't afford it" when they followed up with student families after the financial aid award packages were received. In our shop, the admission and financial aid teams collaborated and cross-trained in the process and options to realize when to "negotiate." As the Admission Counselors worked with the student and family from initial interest through acceptance and admission to the institution, it was critical (in my philosophy) for the Counselor to review the award package with the family. This is where the value of the institution is typically defined (benefits perceived vs. bottom-line cost). When a family felt the perceived value wasn't there or had a "better" deal, we offered them the opportunity to appeal. A simple form was created to complete and justify their appeal and any circumstances we needed to consider. Forwarded through the Counselor to the Appeals Committee (Vice President of Enrollment, Dean of Admission and Director of Financial Aid), the student's profile was prepared by that student's Admission Counselor (GPA, EFC, discount rate, etc.) with their recommendation regarding the appeal and why. We reviewed appeals weekly and responded to each student with an official letter of decision and fiscal response. Each follow up was personal and reinforced with our institution's benefits and our desire for the student to enroll. LRAP was used in this strategy and offered as a unique benefit we provided.

LRAP was used in this strategy and offered as a unique benefit we provided.

However, the buy-in on this novel strategy was needed throughout the campus community for success to be realized. Admission staff would need training to articulate the benefits of LRAP in concert with selling the college product. The Financial Aid staff needed training as well to ensure the awarding of aid included LRAP as part of the institution's investment in the student's education. Advancement and Development needed to be convinced this wonderful "safety-net" the college was providing students was a fundraising opportunity for donors who wanted to help students in a meaningful way.

The program needed consistent and effective marketing. We covered all of these components when implementing the LRAP strategy. The initial step in building an enrollment partnership with Ardeo was to implement the LRAP strategy in our appeals process. Utilized in this way, we were able to secure 14 new students considering other offers. For a college the size of E&H, this was significant! This impact opened doors to additional options for consideration, including aggressive follow-up to uncommitted new students in the applicant pool after May 1. This option was very attractive as Ardeo would shoulder the work of contacting and identifying students interested in our college and LRAP. Then they would hand off the prospect to the institutional staff. Ardeo once again demonstrated the importance of working with our institution on diverse strategies to support enrollment stability while providing a meaningful benefit for students entering college.

My history of working with Ardeo, and the LRAP strategy, may be a bit different than others in this book. I left E&H for retirement soon after the LRAP appeal process was implemented. Without an internal champion on campus working with the Ardeo team, strategies with Ardeo in support of enrollment health waned rather than grew, resulting in a return to enrollment stress. Had I remained at E&H, I would have recommended embellished use of LRAP for students enrolling at the institution. However, we still achieved significant results with the program. We split-tested LRAPs for financial aid appeals and had a 50% yield increase over the non-LRAP cohort of the same year. We also had 43 additional students enroll with LRAP over two years. A survey indicated 76% of students reported LRAP positively influenced their decision to enroll.

> As a vendor to colleges seeking a strategy to set them apart from the competition, this approach makes Ardeo a meaningful player in higher education today and for all the right reasons.

There are a variety of strategic ways to use LRAP with various student cohorts that almost all institutions are trying to either grow or stabilize. When using data analytics, the institutions can determine students less likely to enroll early in the process and offer the LRAP strategically in the recruitment process. Knowing the challenges in recruiting out-of-state students, consider offering LRAP to this cohort. With financial aid information readily available, EFC can determine recipients of the benefit focusing on high need—knowing the career salary levels in many of the liberal arts programs offer the benefit to these declared majors (education, ministry, etc.). With retention, a key component of enrollment stability, look to the third-semester student profiles of high attrition and offer the opportunity before the summer during the second semester. There were a host of strategic options LRAP could provide to enhance a long-term plan at a college willing to be nimble in meeting the challenges of enrollment. These strategies were all in the holster when my retirement called.

A survey indicated 76% of students reported LRAP positively influenced their decision to enroll.

If you are considering working with Ardeo, I have two recommendations. First, make sure you comprehensively understand the many benefits this product brings to the campus beyond the hope of "more freshmen" enrolling. Second, discuss, across campus, the potential opportunities Ardeo can bring to your university: new freshmen, new transfers, returning sophomores, specific majors, specific profiles, negotiating parents, advancement/ fundraising opportunity, brand enhancement, students on the fence in June, parents' council support, more graduates, etc. If there is perceived virtue and benefit outside of the admission and enrollment division, the approval process for needed funds is improved. Just get all the folks in one room.

I continue to support and recommend Ardeo to institutions with which I have contacts. Since my introduction to LRAP eight years ago, I have witnessed the growth of Ardeo and the breadth of strategies they now offer to each campus. Beyond the strategies they provide, they also partner with the admission team to perform the "grunt work" of working with the database of potential students that many small colleges don't have enough hours for. As a vendor to colleges seeking a strategy to set them apart from the competition, this approach makes Ardeo a meaningful player in higher education today and for all the right reasons.

CHAPTER 10

THE NO-RISK FAULKNER APPROACH

KEITH MOCK
FAULKNER UNIVERSITY

F aulkner University is a great Christian college with a close-knit campus community, successful alumni and gifted professors who genuinely care about their students' success. As a private, Christian university, we measured ourselves by the strength of our traditional program, but our other programs— including our long-standing adult program and our emerging graduate programs—funded much of our budget.

We also target the traditional population of students associated with the church of Christ—the faith tradition of the University.

Located in Alabama's capital city of Montgomery, Faulkner's location can be viewed as both a blessing and a curse. There are abundant opportunities for students involving rich cultural experiences and a wide range of internships. Unfortunately, internships aren't the only opportunities offered; so are the options among colleges. Nine out of Faulkner's top 11 competitors are

ABOUT THE AUTHOR: Keith Mock is the former Vice President for Enrollment Management at Faulkner University in Montgomery, AL, where he served for more than 26 years. He has spent his entire career in higher education and specializes in helping colleges and universities formulate and execute creative marketing strategies. Keith holds a bachelor's degree from Faulkner University and doctorate from Capella University.

low-cost state schools or community colleges. Exacerbating the comparative cost issue is that many students, even those who lived near the University, had never heard of us. Even worse, some did not perceive a Faulkner education as prestigious. It is an unknown and, therefore, an underappreciated and misunderstood entity.

Still, our name buys and communication flows were solid. We traveled as we should and kept the phone lines hot. Admissions counselors were continuously trained. The entire campus visit experience was well-rehearsed, and professors knew to greet the families warmly as they walked the campus with our ambassadors. Even so, the competitive world of college admissions demands that every advantage be exploited and every weakness addressed.

> **Incremental gains in numbers of students who were genuinely targeted—mission fit students—were the ones we wanted to see.**

In this context, we continued to search for marketing or recruiting advantages to make the class. Giant leaps in enrollment numbers would be fantastic, such as those we saw with added athletic programs and other specific student activities. However, incremental gains in numbers of students who were genuinely targeted—mission-fit students—were the ones we wanted to see. The basics of recruiting were covered, but were we doing all that we could? Every member of our enrollment team knew the School's value proposition had to dramatically improve if we were going to succeed.

Like many, if not most private colleges, Faulkner is dependent on tuition revenue to drive the funding of the annual operating budget. The Advancement Office and the fundraisers at most institutions receive a lot of attention and resources. Still, the Enrollment Office and the Admissions personnel's tireless work makes it possible to operate effectively since a large percentage of the operating budget comes from student tuition. Our very survival was dependent on enrolling an adequate number of students each year. Fortunately, our revenue streams were diverse and included adult, graduate and online programs in addition to the flagship on-campus traditional program. The existence of multiple revenue streams did not seem to matter, especially to the donors; the traditional program must be strong, and those mission-fit students must enroll.

The competition factor, coupled with our weak market position, made it challenging to attract the number of students needed to keep funding at optimal levels. We were always looking for tools to assist us in enrolling a critical mass of students. Over the years, we tried several different initiatives with varying success.

> **Changing the campus conversation around financial aid was vital in moving forward with the adoption of LRAP.**

We began by purchasing a high-powered Customer Relationship Management (CRM) tool and acquired a partnership with an industry-leading marketing firm. This was the first time we had ever automated the admissions communications and workflow. It made life easier for our counselors and helped the leadership by providing several management tools. It also allowed us to address our value proposition by presenting the Faulkner experience in a more sophisticated and exciting way. We were pleased with the marginal enrollment gains we experienced as a result, although they soon reached a plateau. It seemed that even when the correct number and type of students were placed at the top of the enrollment funnel, several factors kept them from enrolling. We noted that conversion rates at the lower end of the funnel seemed to drop off, and the May 1 benchmark date became more stressful.

During this time of re-tooling, concurrent initiatives in strategic pricing and tuition discounting were also occurring. For the first time, tuition prices were set in advance of the coming year, and formal cost comparatives were considered essential regarding our competitors and aspirational schools. Additionally, enrollment management was tasked with developing and implementing a new scholarship model that had, at its core, the intent of increasing net-tuition revenue. Approaching the building of a financial aid model from the lens of maximizing net-tuition revenue helped us maintain our priority. This gave us opportunities to help others shift their existing traditional paradigms about financial aid to one that made foundational business sense—if the student doesn't enroll, the school does not receive tuition dollars. While orienting an institution's financial aid strategy around the increase of net revenue may sound intuitive, changing the campus conversation around financial aid was vital in moving forward with the adoption of LRAP. These conversations helped to shape an ideology that later guided the way we configured the awarding of LRAP.

This paradigm shift influenced us to think more creatively about recruiting initiatives.

Before the genesis of the new scholarship initiatives, our recruiters (and many in the administration) perceived our scholarship funds as a finite amount in a budget line item. Furthermore, numerous scholarships, under various names, were granted to individual students, significantly decreasing the students' net-revenue rate. Interestingly, these were usually the students who were both willing and able to pay for a Faulkner education. In essence, we were overpaying for the very students who would enroll if given a smaller aid package. On the other side of the coin, we were bound by onerous scholarship guidelines that prohibited us from granting additional institutional aid to students who just needed a little extra funding to attend. We regularly let students who would have brought $12,000 in net revenue cancel their applications and enroll elsewhere just because we could not step outside the established scholarship parameters and offer the funding needed to bridge the gap. The average annual net revenue per student at that time was around $11,000, so we needed those students who were regularly leaving us and enrolling elsewhere.

Thankfully, the new scholarship paradigm allowed for flexibility in awarding. Utilizing this new structure, we began to see the benefits of being agile and elastic in our award process; incremental gains were occurring. We met all or part of a student's demonstrated need as computed by our internal formulas. Discussions about recruiting a particular student began to revolve around the net revenue students would bring in rather than the amount of money in scholarships they would "cost us" to enroll.

This paradigm shift influenced us to think more creatively about recruiting initiatives. It allowed us as a leadership team to consider options that—until that time—would have been immediately dismissed. Just because the environment was more open than it had been traditionally, it did not necessarily mean that we could quickly begin making decisions. Usually, institutions make decisions with glacial speed, and we had only started to improve our ability to change processes deftly.

LRAPs help our prospective students and their parents see how much we believe in the value of a Faulkner education.

It was serendipitous that we first learned of the existence of LRAP in this environment. Even so, helping the CFO and others fully grasp the concept of LRAP was challenging at best. Most of the questions that stood between us and launching the project revolved around the structure of the tool, the stability of the company's financial backing and how would we use the tool in a way that would be affordable to the University.

Our Ardeo representative had already become a trusted advisor. In a series of meetings, he skillfully addressed concerns from our legal counsel and others about the Company's financial solvency and the methodology behind repaying students for the loan payments they made. With those concerns at bay, we turned our attention to the methods of awarding LRAP. How could we install this solution without straining an already perilous budget?

As internal discussions among leadership developed, it became clear that LRAP was the right tool for us in many ways:

- There was no out-of-pocket cost for students.
- The Institution only paid when it worked (students enrolled and borrowed, proving the need for an LRAP).
- Ardeo did not have any hidden fees.
- LRAPs eased student loan debt concerns.
- LRAPs helped our prospective students and their parents see how much we believe in the value of a Faulkner education.

Enrollment Management was convinced that Ardeo's LRAPs could fulfill this tall order; we just needed to be creative in deploying it. After the discussion began, the contract was signed, and in only a few weeks, we deployed this new and exciting tool.

Our structure for awarding LRAP the first couple of years was very conservative. Consistent with the way several other schools began with LRAP, we awarded it only to students in the very late stages of the admission process, which indicated they could not attend due to financial reasons. Instead of offering extra scholarship money, in many cases, we offered LRAP to them. Our fee for enrolling them in LRAP was usually less than the scholarship amount it would have taken to convince them to enroll. Using this approach, we gained 5-6 students each year. While this may not sound like many students, it was an excellent addition to an incoming class that usually ran around 350 and netted an additional $55,000 to $65,000 each year.

> As internal discussions among leadership developed, it became clear that LRAP was the right tool for us in many ways.

We only offered LRAP to those students who would not otherwise have enrolled. This strategy ensured that LRAP was 100% responsible for their enrollment at Faulkner during the time it was used and that we gained the net revenue brought in by the student. The earlier conversations about concentrating on net revenue instead of tuition discounts were key to the leadership accepting this paradigm. Enrollment Management and the CFO had a running debate about whether the fee paid to Ardeo should be considered a straight cost or lumped in with the tuition discount rate figures. She felt the fees incurred should be accounted for as part of the unfunded discount rate. Either way, we knew that using LRAP to yield a student meant we gained net revenue that would not have otherwise been there.

After piloting the program, we realized LRAP was a versatile tool and could have a more substantial impact on our ability to yield our class. We were committed to maintaining the initial intent of the LRAP utilization; we would only use it when assured the student would not matriculate otherwise. Using it in this way would not add a liability to the budget. Through some internal meetings and brainstorming sessions that also included our trusted LRAP advisor, we began to cast our gaze on those students who were in the upper levels of the enrollment funnel.

Our fee for enrolling them in LRAP was usually less than the scholarship amount it would have taken to convince them to enroll.

The "Faulkner Approach," as it became known at Ardeo (and later renamed the Stale Funnel Approach) was developed around the "no risk" sentiment. We gave our best shot at recruiting prospective students at every stage in the funnel through targeted, multi-channel marketing efforts appropriate for their level of interest. Using historical research on prospective students' behavior in previous years, coupled with current intel gained from the Admissions Counselors, helped us determine—within a reasonable range—the point at which students at various stages lost interest in pursuing a Faulkner education. In our net-tuition revenue paradigm, those students were a lost cause. It did not matter if we offered a reasonable amount of additional aid or the enrollment in an LRAP since they would not bring in any revenue if they didn't enroll. Within reasonable limits, some tuition revenue is better than none.

Four low-yield groups were chosen for this approach:

1. We included inquiries who still had not applied for admission even after receiving our multi-channel cadence. Since we kicked off this "no-lose" campaign in late spring, we were reasonably assured these students would not apply.

2. We turned to the population of students who had applied but never completed their applications. This process was somewhat manual because we had to avoid including varsity athletes or others who intended to enroll but had not completed their paperwork.

3. We chose to target those students who had submitted a FAFSA but had not chosen to apply for admission.

4. We included students who had been admitted and had

completed a FAFSA but had not deposited.

For us, the proper timing to run a campaign of this nature was shortly after our May 1 soft deadline for commitment.

We were aided in our approach with marketing collateral provided by Ardeo and information sent out through our CRM. Our measured, multi-channel approach reached both students and their parents. We quickly followed up with students when they showed interest and worked to overcome their objections, which, of course, usually revolved around tuition cost or loan aversion. A portion of our messaging was intended to help with our value proposition. After all, if we believed in a Faulkner education so much that we could guarantee that a graduate could either attain a job shortly after graduation with a very competitive salary or receive loan repayment assistance, there must be some inherent value.

The "Faulkner Approach," as it became known at Ardeo (and later renamed the Stale Funnel Approach) was developed around the "no risk" sentiment.

We were rewarded with our efforts in the inaugural year of the "no-lose" stale funnel approach. We increased the enrollment by 22 students, which represented a 3.5% increase in the freshman class. This increase was nothing short of exceptional because each of these students had crossed Faulkner off their list based on their lack of responsiveness before the LRAP offer. They also possessed outstanding educational credentials and had multiple admission and scholarship offers at various schools. Due to the success of this approach, the stale funnel initiative became a staple in the annual recruitment plan. We became more mindful about how particular students moved through the funnel throughout the year, and we became better at targeting our lists.

The next iteration of LRAP usage came as we continued to see its efficacy in the stale funnel approach. We noted that many students and parents valued their enrollment in LRAP at a higher level than receiving a small institutional scholarship. It was evident that LRAPs were more effective in winning the prospective student's and their parent's hearts and minds than an incremental institutional award. Noting this reality, we substituted an LRAP Award for additional institutional aid for as many students as possible. We did this frequently when the stale funnel approach was needed to yield the student. Even so, we fell short of marketing the program to the masses. It was not advantageous for us to award LRAPs to all students, but we desired to make LRAP Awards a larger part of our outreach earlier in the year.

Conversations with this group of students began to shift from cost to value, and we started to matriculate these students, who usually would have gone to one of our competitors.

How could we be more far-reaching and proactive in early marketing and still keep our financial exposure at a low level? Again, we brainstormed and turned to the Ardeo professionals for advice. In doing so, we realized that we were making an automatic award of $1,000 per year to each student who was a member of the church of Christ. As internal discussions among leadership developed, it became clear that LRAP was the right tool for us—in many ways.

The church of Christ is our faith tradition. Students belonging to it were the most sought after, best-fit students and those we valued to the degree that this long-standing, automatic award was made available exclusively to them. Interestingly, the market lift we received from this discount had diminished over time as each year it became a smaller percentage of the overall cost of attendance. What if we ceased awarding the scholarship and instead provided each student member of the church of Christ an LRAP Award? The amount we spent on the scholarship was almost precisely the same cost as providing an LRAP to the student.

We welcomed this epiphany and could not wait to install the program. It was already late in the recruiting year, but we began offering LRAPs to all new applicants who belonged to this group. Doing so allowed us to heavily market LRAPs to the rising seniors in this group and, of course, to those who were late in making their application for admission.

Replacing the meager scholarship with LRAP for this entire

population of the church of Christ enrollments benefited us in several ways. It gave us the freedom to market this differentiator at large gatherings of our target students. It helped the church of Christ groups feel elevated and desired. They knew we valued and wanted them at our University. Making this investment in students from our faith tradition gave each member of the Faulkner family another proof point that demonstrated that mission attainment was our primary driver. We heavily stressed that the church of Christ student must graduate to take advantage of the loan repayment assistance.

We increased the enrollment by 22 students, which represented a 3.5% increase in the freshman class.

LRAPs' effects on new enrollment and market positioning are pretty straightforward. The Faulkner value proposition took a grand leap forward by marketing to this large affinity group and providing the LRAP promise. From early on, LRAP was 100% effective—students who did enroll with it would not have enrolled otherwise. The pecking order had long been established among this small group of universities as we always competed with our "sister schools" for these particular students. Our conversations with this group of students began to shift from cost to value, and we started to matriculate these students, who usually would have gone to one of our competitors. The percentage of these best-fit students we won increased by 5% year-over-year, effectively bringing in more revenue.

These students shared that LRAPs made the difference in attending Faulkner, their first-choice school, versus having to make other college arrangements. LRAPs provided safety and security while alleviating the stress of trying to figure out how to pay off loans after graduation when starting salaries of first-time jobs were lower.

Faulkner's partnership with Ardeo has been both successful and enjoyable. Ardeo's LRAPs are financially sound, easy to administer and incredibly flexible in deployment methodology. We enjoyed the marketing support as well as the backing and encouragement in creatively administering the program. Both the students and personnel at Faulkner still benefit from the Ardeo partnership, which is now in its seventh year.

CHAPTER 11

SUPPORTING THE MISSION

PJ WOOLSTON & PATRICK VERHILEY
MARIAN UNIVERSITY

M arian University prides itself on being a great Catholic university dedicated to providing excellent teaching and learning in the Franciscan and liberal arts tradition. Marian College (now Marian University since 2009), founded by the Sisters of St. Francis of Oldenburg, moved from Oldenburg, Indiana to Indianapolis, Indiana, in 1937. Over the next 65 years, compelled to act with the virtue of courage, the leadership of this small Indiana college embarked on new adventure after new adventure.

Like with many smaller, faith-based universities, Marian attracts a high number of students who target service-oriented and socially-minded future careers. Consequently, many of these students intend to serve their church (the Catholic church in particular) as lay leaders full-time or in significant volunteer roles.

ABOUT THE AUTHOR: PJ Woolston is the former Vice President for Enrollment Management at Marian University. He has worked in all non-profit sectors of higher education (public, private, two-year, four-year). He has a bachelor's degree from Brigham Young University, a master's degree from the University of Michigan and a doctorate from the University of Southern California.

ABOUT THE AUTHOR: Patrick Verhiley is the Director of Missionary Disciples Institute at Marian University. He has helped grow Marian University's San Damiano Scholarship Program for Church Leadership to a record setting number of enrollees with LRAPs. He holds a bachelor's degree from Marian University.

Many faith-based schools have extracurricular or co-curricular programs designed to foster and enable these aspirations.

In 2002, Marian embarked on one instance of a new adventure directly tied to mission and faith for the students. In the spirit of courage, Marian College applied for and received a significant grant from the Lilly Endowment Inc. to begin the Rebuild My Church initiative. Rebuild My Church, designed to transform the college by integrating the call to theologically explore vocation, influenced nearly every university aspect from its academic offerings to its recruitment.

The leadership of this small Indiana college embarked on new adventure after new adventure.

Within the initiative, there were three key elements:

1. Seminary, education and formation, which became the Bishop Simon Bruté College Seminary.

2. The broader education and formation offered all faculty, staff and students to explore matters of faith, discernment and vocation through the Franciscan tradition lens.

3. The education and formation of lay leaders for the Church, called the San Damiano Scholars Program for Church Leadership. The first two programs are highly specific in terms of funding and direction for the students. Therefore, this chapter will explore the San Damiano Scholars Program for Church Leadership.

The San Damiano Scholars Program for Church Leadership began with intentional recruitment, education and lay leaders' formation for service to the Church in 2003. Inspired by the story of Saint Francis of Assisi and his call to rebuild the church, the program invites young people to consider how God is calling them to rebuild the church today. All scholars pursue a minor in pastoral leadership, including 18 or 19 credits in theology, some of which are cross-discipline courses paired with the student's major. In addition to this academic component, all students engage in the following co-curricular elements: monthly formation meetings, bi-annual retreats, monthly service with theological reflection, spiritual direction, leadership in ministry projects and faith-based internships. Above all, the students are most attracted to journeying through college with a community of like-minded peers passionate about growing in faith. Altogether, the San Damiano Scholarship Program intends to produce the next generation of leaders for the Church.

Indeed, from the beginning, recruitment for future Church leaders became a priority for many on Marian University's campus. The University turned its eyes toward seeking high-achieving young people called to servant leadership. The program began specifically recruiting students who demonstrated intellectual curiosity, openness to God and their neighbors, active leadership in the community and the church, strong interior life rooted in prayer and willingness to live in community. To select the right students, staff developed an in-depth application with faith-related reflection questions and a four-hour interview process involving Marian University faculty, staff and current San Damiano Scholars. Even during the interview process, students made deep connections and began to see they were not alone in loving their faith. After completing the selection process, the San Damiano Scholar staff awarded scholarships to deserving students. Scholarships were selective, and amounts varied up to half-tuition. This was directly relevant because students self-selecting into this program were also choosing careers with parallel priorities, which were generally associated with lower-income levels. Thus, the San Damiano Scholar's scholarships were a critical recruitment tool because they provided immense and necessary financial help and reassurance for anyone considering work in the church upon graduation.

The San Damiano Scholars program was also intended to be an enrollment driver for the University. Staff at Marian knew that the program would start relatively small, but the goal ultimately was to grow the incoming San Damiano class to 50 students. In the inaugural class, Marian invited 15 students to be San Damiano Scholars. At this point in Marian's history, the first-time, full-time

> From the beginning, recruitment for future Church leaders became a priority for many on Marian University's campus.

freshmen numbered 236, with San Damiano Scholars making up just over 6% of the class. In the early stages of the program, the University operated out of the grant funds from the Lilly Endowment Inc. Over the next 12 years, enrollment in the San Damiano Program varied between 25-35 students per class. The staff had hit a plateau for recruiting students for such a specific program, and it became increasingly clear that they needed to make some changes. This was particularly clear concerning cost. With each passing year, the scholarship's relative value diminished as tuition and room and board increased while the scholarship amounts remained constant.

> An alternative to the popular discourse of eliminating or reducing student loan debt was managing that debt in more healthy ways that were beneficial to all parties.

While the cost of a private university education was an obvious challenge, this was a hurdle faced by all Marian prospective students. Like many private schools, Marian has a listed tuition that can be intimidating at first glance, but the market position for that tuition figure complicates recruitment in interesting ways. Since enrollment competition will always be defined at least to some extent geographically, even while Marian's brand and academic profile have improved, its primary competitor institutions have at least included other private schools in Indiana. In terms of tuition, Marian faces direct competition on either side of its tuition price point. On one side are private schools with a similar profile (relatively small, frequently religiously affiliated, NAIA or NCAA Division II/III athletics, etc.) where tuition is 15% to 20% lower (e.g., under $30,000 compared to Marian in the low to mid-$30,000 level). On the other side are private schools with a broader profile and a more selective market position (usually more prominent, more national draw, NCAA Division I athletics, etc.) where tuition is significantly higher (i.e., in the mid-$40,000 level). The "sticker price" is often a hurdle even at the application level for all students, let alone at the point-of-decision and enrollment deposit. This is even more the case for students targeting mission-driven careers and church service.

For several years in the mid-2010s, increased discussion of student debt throughout the media generated multiple new and innovative conversations around student loans. An alternative to the popular discourse of eliminating or reducing student loan debt was managing that debt in more healthy ways that were beneficial to all parties. The Loan Repayment Assistance Program (LRAP) offered by Ardeo was one thoughtfully developed approach. Marian had explored the possibility of integrating the idea into their recruitment operation. Still, executive leadership could not come to a consensus as to whether it would be effective for student recruitment and executable for the institutional budget. Most enrollment ideas had centered around reducing the direct cost to students (e.g., more scholarship, tuition reset, etc.), whereas this approach did not address cost at all. Would students respond to a commitment to affordability designed to help them repay student loans rather than minimize them?

Exacerbating the challenge was the fact that Marian had begun to plateau in terms of overall institutional enrollment. Over the previous several years, the incoming class for Marian had reached a plateau, which was reflected in enrollment levels for the San Damiano Scholar's program. Up to this point, the program had not yet achieved the targeted incoming enrollment of 50 students, despite various creative and innovative efforts to do so. Attempts to enhance and strengthen recruitment included expanded staffing, expanded recruitment efforts (more regional recruitment, greater outreach via mail and email, etc.), an organizational restructuring (moving San Damiano Scholars recruitment staff out of the Office of Campus Mission & Ministry and into the Office of Freshman Admissions), and even more generous scholarship amounts despite institutional funding limitations. The process was greatly enhanced so that the application and interview could better serve the recruitment technique.

While headcount and discount rate were always interrelated with San Damiano Scholars enrollment, the staff realized during the 2017-18 recruitment cycle (recruiting the Fall 2018 class) that prospective students with long-term mission-oriented careers and lower expectations for income were becoming increasingly reluctant to commit to the cost of a private education despite the additional programmatic scholarship funding. The Board of Trustees had approved a tuition rate of $34,000. Across the undergraduate population, about one-third of incoming students were Pell-eligible (i.e., relatively high need). Nearly three-quarters of students took out federal loans to help fund their education. Marian's overall discount rate had become relatively high (higher than the national average for small private schools). Despite the effort to keep student debt down to manageable levels, the Marian staff found they had reached a limit in terms of the amount of aid they could offer admitted students while still generating enough tuition revenue to operate a high-quality program. This was even more the case for institutionally prioritized students like those in the San Damiano Scholars program who were more highly leveraged.

> Up to this point, the program had not yet achieved the targeted incoming enrollment of 50 students, despite various creative and innovative efforts to do so.

A more in-depth conversation about LRAP emerged in the middle of the cycle (January to February). It became more apparent than it had previously that this would be of value to the San Damiano Scholar population. As the President's Cabinet debated and discussed the possibilities and implications, it resonated on many levels. The Provost appreciated the connection between the financial model (reducing risk for the student) and prioritizing student success (not having to worry as much about the finances). The President wanted to learn more about the principle, including its feasibility and the risks involved. He was so impressed with the model that he wondered whether it needed to be managed externally or if Marian could do it independently. While certainly a possibility, Marian quickly realized that the cost of developing, implementing and maintaining a program would be prohibitively high, even if only in terms of staffing, not to mention accounting liability. If Marian wanted to commit to helping students manage their loan repayment in this way, they would need help.

The CFO recognized and immediately pointed out that the LRAP approach mitigated risk for everyone. Students had lower pressure on immediate post-graduation income, knowing their payments would be covered. The institution only paid a premium for students who borrowed—meaning payment was directly tied to enrollment success. An external partner who was an expert in the field could navigate the arrangement and long-term tracking details.

After thoroughly vetting it, the President and his cabinet approved the partnership, and the Office of Admissions immediately began the rollout to supplement the scholarship program already in place. Promotion was particularly delicate. Marian was only offering participation in the LRAP program to incoming freshmen who enrolled in the San Damiano Scholars program, not the entire freshman class. They coordinated carefully with the Admission Counselors and the financial aid office to ensure that these counselors understood and could represent the details of what LRAP was, how it was being managed and who qualified for it. The counselors who primarily benefitted from the new initiative were the recruiters specific to the San Damiano Scholars program. Where Admission Counselors were taking care to ensure that they only addressed the possibility of LRAP for the relevant population, the San Damiano Scholars recruiters could talk about it much more freely since it was applicable for their entire admitted student population. Further, no additional application or fee was necessary; any enrolling student who borrowed would automatically be enrolled.

> The LRAP program became a significant added value that many students actually called, "a gift from Marian."

The response was tremendously positive. Some families had no intention of taking out student loans, so the question was moot; however, there was an extra measure of assurance in the program even for those families. It gave them an even greater degree of confidence in Marian University, the school to which they were about to commit the next four years of their life. On the other hand, and more importantly, for students who needed the additional aid from student loans, this was the "icing on the cake." The LRAP program became a significant added value that many students actually called, "a gift from Marian."

The program's value only grew in subsequent cycles as the staff had more time to make LRAP a standard part of San Damiano recruitment. For the Fall 2018 cycle, LRAP was offered late in the recruitment cycle, almost as a bonus.

LRAP has empowered the University to better meet its mission of lifting society both on the individual and societal levels.

The following year once LRAP had become standard for San Damiano Scholars and the staff were recruiting the Fall 2019 class, they were able to lead with LRAP as yet another tool among many (noting preeminently nature and quality of the San Damiano Scholars curriculum). For many students in the Fall 2018 class, LRAP was "the" difference-maker, making it possible for them to commit to their first-choice school. For students in the Fall 2019 class, LRAP was "a" difference-maker, becoming an essential part of a bigger picture.

As a result, incoming student enrollment in Fall 2018 finally grew for the first time to exceed the initial goal set over a decade earlier of 50 students. This San Damiano Scholars class numbered 55 out of the entire freshman class of 424. Even for the Fall 2019 class, when overall enrollment at Marian took a slight downturn to 386, San Damiano Scholars enrollment only contracted down to the goal number of 50, something that would have been a dream situation just a few years earlier.

Marian immediately realized one other important element that loan repayment assistance was playing with San Damiano Scholars. Because of participation in LRAP, retention for the program climbed even higher, exceeding 90% for the first time in program history, well above the University average. This is an important reflection of the overall goal of Marian University. While Marian has many goals, including enrollment, retention, net-tuition revenue, and so forth, the ultimate overriding institutional priority is the number of degrees granted in any given year. All other numbers contribute to this most important metric, the number of college degrees, which is the true driver of upward socioeconomic mobility and the real measure of higher-education success. At Marian, loan repayment assistance has amply demonstrated its utility as a critical tool enhancing student confidence in the University and empowering student commitment to a lifelong service to their chosen calling.

> **Because of participation in LRAP, retention for the program climbed even higher, exceeding 90% for the first time in program history, well above the University average.**

More importantly, it has empowered the University to better meet its mission of lifting society both on the individual and societal levels. More people graduate from college, allowing them better and more fulfilling jobs with higher levels of income. Those same graduates go throughout Indiana and the surrounding states, where they lift the communities around them through their work. Further, experiencing such immediate and positive results from a loan repayment assistance partnership has compelled Marian to consider how the school can extend this opportunity to its entire population.

CHAPTER 12

LCU ADVANTAGE: ATTACKING AN AUDACIOUS GOAL

MONDY BREWER
LUBBOCK CHRISTIAN UNIVERSITY

All seemed well. I had 11 years of combined experience in Enrollment Management, Marketing, Admissions, Financial Assistance, Retention and a PhD in Leadership, when I made a career move away from the "Dark Side" and became a graduate faculty member. Five years on the teaching side of higher education was completed.

All seemed well until the new University President, in his second year, saw trouble on the horizon. New student recruitment was suffering. The Admissions team realized a 21% decrease in new student recruiting. The team was breaking apart. The Director and Vice President both resigned. The University needed help. I was called on by the Executive Leadership Team to assist in finding a new Vice President for Enrollment Management. A national search failed; long story short, I was asked to take up the mantle again. I was up for the challenge.

ABOUT THE AUTHOR: Mondy Brewer is the Vice President of Client Service at Ardeo Education Solutions. He is the former Vice President of Enrollment Management at Lubbock Christian University. He holds a doctorate, master's degree and bachelor's degree from Lubbock Christian University.

Many new hires and fires within the Admissions team were immediately needed. This included onboarding an unexperienced Director with high character. After the team started to settle, the President decided to give my team and me a new goal: make up the 21% loss but also increase first-time-full-time (FTFT) freshmen by 25%. "You have three years to do it," he said.

Lubbock Christian University (LCU) is in Lubbock, Texas, located literally across the street from another great institution of higher learning, Texas Tech University. Lubbock is a college town of about 300,000 people, 50,000 of whom are college students. LCU was founded in 1957 by members of the churches of Christ. They came together to establish a Christian university on the South Plains of Texas to prepare and equip students for Christian service lives. LCU has approximately 2,500 students, 300 of whom are graduate students. The university is known for its nursing school and school of education, which boasts 100% employment of its graduates year after year. Each year, the Admission team is expected to bring in approximately 320 new FTFT freshman students while averaging more than 200 transfer and readmit students.

Make up the 21% loss but also increase first-time-full-time (FTFT) freshmen by 25%. "You have three years to do it," he said.

The Fall 2015 recruiting class—my first year back—saw a 34% increase in FTFT freshman students. Strategic hiring, along with "back to basics" recruiting practices brought LCU's new student enrollment back to a stable and comfortable place. "However, falling birth rates, negative media portrayals, and changing student loyalties and preferences presented stark challenges to colleges and universities' leaders," according to an *Enrollment Management Report, 19: 3-3 What keeps enrollment managers up at night?* In my five years as a faculty member, a lot had changed. Lubbock Christian University was not immune to these phenomena. The audacious goal was going to prove difficult. I was going to have to re-think what I knew about enrollment management, specifically recruiting.

I was Vice President for Enrollment at a small Christian

university in Texas. We were bleeding students to the large research institution down the street and the junior college 40 miles away. Our audacious goal was public knowledge across campus, and we had to succeed. I was obviously looking for ideas.

As I began looking for new initiatives or concepts to help fill the funnel, I attended a conference of schools like LCU in September after that first year back "in the saddle." An old colleague and friend of mine, from a small Christian school in Alabama, presented some positions and plans they were employing in an attempt to "move the needle" in the very competitive Southern region. While presenting, he mentioned using LRAPs in conjunction with supplemental scholarships to drive yield. I wasn't exactly sure what he was talking about. I felt like I was the only one in the room who didn't know about LRAPs.

One thing that became obvious to me in that first year back in the VPE seat was the number of debt-averse families.

Most people who lead enrollment teams tend to have a FOMO (Fear of Missing Out) mentality regarding recruiting. I was no exception to this rule. Rather than look foolish and ask the question in front of the group, I talked with my friend about it over dinner that evening. I immediately saw the potential this product might give to a university's recruiting effort. The words "promise," "safety" and "guarantee" kept coming up in the conversation, which was intriguing. I rarely reached out to a vendor—I mostly despised them—but this case was different. I asked my friend for contact information, and within a few short days, I met face-to-face with a representative from Ardeo who explained in great detail how LRAPs could help my yield and impact my audacious goal. I was skeptical but optimistic about the possibilities.

One thing that became obvious to me in that first year back in the VPE seat was the number of debt-averse families. I remember meeting with a family who told me there was no way their son would be able to take on $70,000 in debt for a bachelor's degree at LCU. This shocked me since the average borrowing rate at LCU was about $37,000. What was more shocking was the hypocritical fact that this same family was making payments on an $80,000+ automobile that was sitting in one of our visitor's parking spaces outside my window. It seemed that the vehicle was essential—a bachelor's degree, to them, was not.

It appeared that a large number of families had an inflated misunderstanding regarding the amount of borrowing that would be required for a bachelor's degree at LCU according to LCU's participation in the National Survey of Student Engagement. I soon realized they were getting their information mainly from the news media who tend to report the extreme cases rather than the average. In 2019, the average media story reported a bachelor's degree borrowing rate at $85,400. Additionally, many families I engaged also follow a popular debt elimination plan that is very popular in the south. It teaches that borrowing for something like a college degree is foolish. One family said, "The program says get it [a bachelor's degree] as cheap as possible." While I agree with most of this system's ideas and concepts, I disagree that borrowing for college is a poor investment. I argue that it is a better investment than a home—which is the only thing this program says borrowing is suitable for according to the *New York Times*, 5/27/14. However, perception is reality.

> **The local "buzz" was significant. Our application counts shot up. We had record highs in almost all funnel categories despite the university's audacious goal across the street.**

I was a skeptic, but I decided to propose the LRAP idea to LCU's Executive Vice President, my boss. I specifically made this decision because the risk of trying the program was low. Since there is no minimum or maximum spend required per year, invoices are determined based only on students who sign their LRAP Award and enroll and borrow, and payment was not due until after my census date, so the consequences seemed small. I was pleased with that. After discussing these merits, the EVP was willing to allow me to give the idea a chance. I was determined to take as little risk as possible that first year, offering it to only about 15 students. I was determined to see proof of a statistically significant concept before

I would invest out of my already tight budgets.

After consultation with Ardeo staff, my strategy would be to offer LRAPs to students who our team determined were very likely to melt. I alleged this approach was very low risk, especially the way I decided we would deploy. Admission Counselors would bring me cases where students were "on the fence," and rather than offer more discounts, I would offer LRAP. The Counselor had to prove there was a need and that probabilities were high that an LRAP offer would yield a deposit. We also looked at offering this to any prospective student who was appealing their financial aid package. Again, the attempt was to keep discounting under control. This is how I planned to prove or disprove the concept. If we were able to get this very small group to deposit, great. If not, then, as I mentioned before, there was no cost to LCU. I looked at the many Ardeo services similarly to having an additional Admission Counselor helping us with a few of our tough "fence-sitting" applicants.

Results that last year were solid, and over the five years "back in the saddle," LCU increased its new student recruiting by 27%.

Year two of my tenure as VPE ended very positively. We were again going to keep the progression moving forward toward our audacious goal. Every funnel category was up, and it appeared that our LRAP experiment was working. Skepticism prevailed even though we had 17 students sign up for the program, 11 of whom borrowed, and three indicated they would not have attended without their LRAP Award. I believed there was enough positive evidence to try the selective plan the next year. I felt we needed supplementary numbers to prove the result was statistically significant. I decided to test it again in similar fashion another year. I knew I could not invest significant dollars on what might just be a one-year anomaly.

Another year with the same "selective" plan revealed similar results. Year three of my tenure as VPE ended very positively. We were again going to keep the progression moving forward toward our audacious goal. Every funnel category was again trending up, and it again appeared our LRAP experiment was working.

My skepticism was diminishing even with 15 students signed up for the program, 12 who were borrowers. The Ardeo student survey revealed that six of those students said they would not have enrolled without the offer of the LRAP. I felt we needed more supplementary numbers to prove the results were significant and not a back-to-back anomaly.

My advice to the Admission team has always been to "do what others can't or won't."

I began year three with the same "selective" plan as the first two years. This year, the difference was that we had some turnover in the Admission Office, plus the large research institution had its own audacious goal—increase its freshman class by 10%. They employed a marketing campaign that was significantly impacting our funnel. This university is our number one competitor, and they had enough marketing money/power to considerably disrupt our audacious goal. Their plan was working, and by the time we got to March of that third year, it was evident that it would be a struggle just to keep pace with the previous year.

My advice to the Admission team has always been to "do what others can't or won't." It was now time for me to "practice what I preached." I decided to offer LRAPs much more broadly in this ninth hour. We not only offered them selectively, as previously, but I also asked Admission Counselors to bring me names of all accepted students who had gone silent. If they were no longer responding to our messaging, we would make an LRAP offer in an attempt to keep pace with the previous recruiting year.

LCU had 61 students sign up for the program that year; 39 were borrowers. The Ardeo student survey revealed that 11 of those students said they would not have enrolled without the offer of an LRAP. I believed we now had enough data to prove the program works.

LRAP helped us increase yield three years in a row! In year three, we were able to prevent a catastrophic recruiting result mainly because we decided to move to a more aggressive posture regarding LRAP offers. We could not make more progress to reach our audacious goal, but we did not lose ground.

My skepticism was now completely gone! I was all in. We were going to offer LRAP to all freshmen except our nursing students. A significant marketing campaign would begin despite reservations from our Director of Financial Assistance and the President. LCU renamed the program The LCU Advantage, complete with its own logo and branding to more broadly disseminate the plan to all our prospective students. Initially, the plan worked perfectly. Local news outlets interviewed our President and me.

LRAP helped us increase yield three years in a row!

The local "buzz" was significant. Our application counts shot up. We had record highs in almost all funnel categories despite the university's audacious goal across the street.

Offering an LRAP to such a large number of students seemed very risky to some of my colleagues on campus. I agreed that the invoices were likely to be large for a school LCU's size, but I could not get past the return on investment I saw the previous three years. It was apparent to me; I expected that we would break even monetarily while seeing significant yield increases.

In 2019, LCU saw many changes again. The President who issued our goal—25% increase in FTFT freshman students— announced his departure. The university across the street still had its own audacious goal that impacted our ability to recruit despite going "all in" with Ardeo. Additionally, I was being recruited by two higher education companies that I highly respected. After over 20 years in higher education, I considered leaving university life and becoming a vendor—something I swore I would never do.

Recruiting continued, and by the spring of the fourth year, it was obvious that we were on pace to have another solid recruiting year. The 2019 school year saw 240 students sign up for the program, 190 were borrowers; the Ardeo student survey revealed that 39 of those students said they would not have enrolled without the LRAP offer. The engagement and dedication from Ardeo staff to ensure our success was overwhelming. They seemed to be different from any vendor I had worked with before. I believed they genuinely had my—and LCU's—best interest in mind.

I discovered the 2019 results from a distance; however, as I accepted a position with Ardeo—the Company I had gained so much respect for—I began serving students and their families from a different perspective on June 4, 2019.

LCU increased its new student recruiting by 27%.

Results that last year were solid, and over the five years "back in the saddle," LCU increased its new student recruiting by 27%. We did not reach the audacious goal, but LRAPs have helped set us on the direct path to reaching it.

CHAPTER 13

FAITH FOR THE FUTURE

JORDAN GRANT
SEATTLE PACIFIC UNIVERSITY

N estled just outside Seattle, Washington, in a peaceful residential area, close to the unique neighborhoods of Fremont and Ballard, is Seattle Pacific University (SPU). It's a private Christian liberal arts university fully committed to engaging in the culture and changing the world by graduating people of competence and character, becoming people of wisdom and modeling a grace-filled community. SPU is also a place of academic rigor within the bustle of the Pacific Northwest's economic engine. For the fourth year in a row, SPU was named a 2020 "Best National University" and one of the top national universities for diversity by *U.S. News and World Report*. Founded in 1891 by Free Methodist pioneers, who valued and sought to create a space for all who seek academic excellence and to change the world for good, SPU is a place where 4,000 students gain a superb education and the tools to influence the world.

As a private, four-year, nonprofit university, SPU is a tuition-dependent institution where undergraduate enrollment drives

ABOUT THE AUTHOR: Jordan Grant is the Associate Vice President for Enrollment Operations and Student Financial Services at Seattle Pacific University. He has spent his entire career in higher education. As a first-generation student, Jordan knows firsthand the challenges of pursuing higher education; he feels grateful to be able to support students' opportunity to "dream out loud." Jordan holds a bachelor's degree from the University of Oregon and a master's degree from Seattle University.

much of the revenue to deliver a nationally ranked education. SPU's tuition in 2019-20 was $44,604 after an increase from the year before. SPU is associated with the Council for Christian Colleges and Universities (CCCU), which includes Christian-based institutions around the country and the world. Although SPU faces stiff competition for in-state students from a robust public university system and other local private institutions, most are not CCCU schools. Yet, by far, the institution that SPU most competes with for students is the state's flagship university.

The University of Washington – Seattle (UW) is the top institution that SPU admitted students choose to attend rather than SPU. UW, Washington State University and Western Washington University are all public universities and consistently in the top five cross-admit schools each year. As a private, non-state funded university, SPU cannot compete with public universities. With a growing concern over student debt and good-paying jobs, students often choose lower-cost schools even if it's not the best fit for them.

The challenging competition from public schools has required us to have superb affordability messaging.

The challenging competition from public schools has required us to have superb affordability messaging. We have worked hard at communicating the robust scholarship and grant programs for students, often targeted to specific groups based on affinity, academic achievements, talent and financial need. Yet, even with the ever-increasing institutional aid expenditures, about two-thirds of SPU graduates must borrow. Our student loan team is dedicated to processing loans and guiding students through the repayment and cancelation maze. This dedicated team's work has led to a three-year cohort default rate under 2% and the average debt amount consistently under $30,000. However, some students still see loans as a barrier, a potential heavyweight grounding their dreams of working in non-profits, education or ministry. We needed a way to strengthen undergraduate enrollment and speak to the growing concern of student debt.

In the early 2010s, we experienced unprecedented enrollment

growth. The average incoming freshman enrollment from 2010-2013 was 759 students; this represented an almost 8% increase in enrollment from the prior three years (2007-2009). For us, this is more than a healthy enrollment; it positioned the institution with strength. Dorms were bursting.

There were questions about classroom space, the need for additional instructors, and how much more the student services and co-curricular programs could handle. The strong enrollment was born out of demographics, SPU's academic programming and competitive financial aid offers. During this time, Washington state and western states saw an increase in college-aged students. There were more students ready to attend the University. We also saw excellent strides in the sciences (nearly 100% of SPU graduates who apply to medical school were accepted), strong School of Education programs respected in the state and other arts and humanities programs. We compared our merit awards with competitors and leveraged targeted additive awards to unique populations such as high-need and high-academic achievers in offering competitive financial offers. Our net revenue was in good shape; we met or exceeded our net-tuition revenue goals for three years straight, and it seemed our strong enrollment and meeting budget goals would go on unabated, albeit with plenty of hard work. Then 2014 hit.

However, some students still see loans as a barrier, a potential heavyweight grounding their dreams of working in non-profits, education or ministry.

At the beginning of the 2014 enrollment cycle, the number of applications and admits was marked closely to 2013 when 767 incoming freshmen said "yes" to SPU. All signs posted were directing us to another banner year of enrollment. Due to stiff private university competition and students' selection of public colleges, a drop in yield across students' spectrum—geography, gender, financial need and academic ability occurred. The effect of the reduction in yield meant SPU missed the headcount, enrolling 685 students, which prompted a recalibration of our admission strategies and the financial aid strategy.

After a decade-plus of operating an institutional financial aid strategy, we contracted with a third-party consultant for the 2015 recruitment cycle. The consultant reviewed the entire admission process for freshmen and transfer students, as well as the financial aid process and institutional aid distribution strategy. The consultant's review of the aid recipients' price sensitivity showed a significant majority of students were price inelastic; in other words, we could offer less financial aid and still achieve enrollment and net-tuition revenue goals. They positioned us to achieve a higher enrollment goal and more net-tuition revenue. Unfortunately, this proved not to be the case.

> One thing I have grown to understand in life—lessons are relearned, again and again.

In the real-world, a non-statistical model, the 2015 freshman class price sensitivity was price elastic—the exact opposite of what the consultant's model demonstrated. The majority of freshmen enrolled at a higher rate when they received additional financial aid; additional students provided a greater likelihood of achieving net-tuition revenue goals. Because of the freshman class's price elasticity, even with +500 more admits than the preview year, enrollment increased just three students to 688. We had designed the aid strategy to offer less funding but expected to achieve headcount and revenue goals. After sitting back, scratching our collective heads, wondering how actual student price sensitivity could shift so dramatically year over year, we saw that losses were found in our largest populated scholarship category, out-of-state admits, and in students who did not qualify for merit awards. Something again needed to change—to be rethought. So, in 2016 the answer seemed to be more aid! This will enroll more students; it was a simple calculation, really.

Beware of what seems simple; human behavior often complicates things. In 2016, the aid strategy allocated additional institutional gift aid to students to influence price-sensitive admits. Also, during this year, the admission strategy changed. It was believed that personalized attention was lost due to the increase in admits the prior year. Admissions deployed a new applicant and admit strategy, which resulted in about 700 fewer admits. This approach included a more strategic and targeted approach in buying student names. Even though the number of applicants was reduced, the admits were believed to be a better fit for our institution. We anticipated a return to the low 20% yield range. The reality did prove a bounce-back in yield but not to the level needed to return to the 700s. We offered additional financial aid to our price-sensitive admits. They were the students who chose SPU. Consequently, the discount rate was higher than projected by 1.5%; 2017 would be different. We learned some lessons (again) and would be better positioned to achieve enrollment and revenue goals.

The LRAP structure allowed us to be in the driver's seat; we could steer where we believed the impact would be the greatest and the most cost-effective.

One thing I have grown to understand in life—lessons are relearned, again and again. In our case, the story of the unforeseen circumstances was told again. In 2017, the aid strategy continued to be modeled with an assumption that admits were primarily price-sensitive, and specific populations required additional aid to feel confident to enroll. The admit count was close to the goal, ending about 250 fewer than projected. The story of how we arrived at the total number of admits in 2017 led us to utilize LRAP.

Leading up to the 2017 enrollment cycle, due to budget constraints and a need to be more administratively streamlined and efficient, some departmental work was consolidated. We merged teams and created a new department—Enrollment Operations. Each staff person was in some way connected to application processing or data and focused more on the processing and data imports and exports. The goal was to streamline processing, create stability and surefootedness in our data. It was the right move; we have seen good efficiencies in process and data, yet unfortunately, there were growing pains. Some high-volume inquiry source data files were not imported into the admission system during the transition of new duties. Although all student inquiries were eventually imported into the system, students did not receive communication as timely as desired. Applications were down 7%. Admits were down 5%. The prospect of meeting the 680s in enrollment numbers was dimly lit, at best. Even achieving the low 600s in enrollment seemed shaky and would push everyone. Something new, something immediate, had to happen.

Around the time of the challenges, Ardeo's Matt Osborne reached out to talk a bit more about the services and impact the Loan Repayment Assistance Program (LRAP) can provide institutions and students. SPU indeed had a problem with a projected significant downturn in enrollment after several years of missing enrollment goals. LRAP was new to our community and could be immediately brought online. We had to move and move quickly.

The concept of LRAP had long intrigued me.

In the Spring of 2017, we were still addressing the enrollment shortfalls experienced in the previous three years. And now, a projected significant drop in applications and admits forecasted a fairly devasting lower enrollment of new freshmen. Something needed to be done. The admissions team went into high(er) gear by launching additional application generation campaigns, offering more aid, reviewing available data and conducting still-active admits. During this time, we received outreach from LRAP staff and promotional materials.

The concept of LRAP had long intrigued me. The idea of providing a safety-net for students concerned about borrowing or those without the extended family wealth and connections to help speaks to the dreams of students looking to serve their community and the world, as well as to significant socioeconomic inequities in the US. Personally, this strikes a chord as well. I was a first-generation student when I started my undergraduate program. I remember distinctly when I received my financial aid award; I looked at the numbers and quickly did the math (first sign that financial aid would be a career for me). The result of my quick calculation was that I could do it; I could go to college. Admission to my university of choice was not the primary hurdle for me—affording it was. This experience marked me in a way that has not left me; I still strive to make the dream of a college degree real for current students. Given my personal reflection on needy students seeking their dreams and our enrollment prospects in 2017, it was time to dig deeper into LRAP to determine if it could help the immediate need.

Typically, a new program that requires a funding source and a third-party contract can be slow-moving as the review process advances through the necessary channels. This moment, though, required a much faster process. LRAP staff, especially Matt Osborne—our Regional LRAP Representative—helped provide several LRAP options. The possibilities were and remain focused on what schools believe will be helpful, can afford or would like to test for effectiveness. Our options seemed wide open. The LRAP structure allowed us to be in the driver's seat; we could steer where we believed the impact would be the greatest and the most cost-effective.

> With LRAP, students go from a scarcity mindset to one of opportunity— the attitude that makes university life full of energy, ideas and possibilities.

We could offer LRAP to these students:

- A select few based on conversations with students and families
- A specific population we believed were in a program with lower earning potential than other programs (such as theology majors)
- Those who had significant concerns about borrowing (such as Pell Grant recipients)
- To all students

Additionally, we could set up acceptance of an LRAP offer to these students:

- Passive (they are recipients—no action needed by the student)
- Active (the student would be required to sign an acceptance within a certain period)

With such flexibility, the power of LRAP, should it be targeted and communicated well, seemed immense and a bit overwhelming. Yet, Matt was clear to mention that LRAP was not a panacea for all our enrollment challenges but could help specific populations.

The discussion of options rested primarily with SPU's Vice President for Enrollment Management and Marketing (VPEMM) and me. We had already increased financial offers for target populations, so the investment in reducing net price was in front of students. Conversations with the VPEMM involved cost, populations and how effective it could be. The discussion was primarily focused on ways we could gain students, which was critical given our position. We decided to engage with LRAP as a pilot program, requiring students to actively accept the offer so that they had a call to action— possibly demonstrating interest in SPU, and targeting populations that we knew could be vulnerable to melt or perceived that attending would require too much borrowing. Before we launch the program, we first needed University Counsel to review the agreement with LRAP.

> In 2017, SPU's first-generation admits began to increase (over 30%) to levels that required targeted attention.

The complexity of legal matters that institutions of higher education must now navigate has created lengthy review processes. Contract review and negotiations can take weeks, if not months, to complete. The VPEMM and I did not believe we had time to wait for the normal process. We could accelerate the review process through specific requests to University Counsel and the possible ramifications of not moving quickly enough—enrollment loss. Strong advocacy from senior leadership, the VPEMM, in this case, is required to move as swiftly as possible and strengthen the legitimacy and reduce the time to market any program. The quick review of this process was no different.

The selection of the populations was not hard to surmise. Staff in admissions and student financial services had challenging discussions with students about debt for years. So, one population we knew we wanted to target was students who expressed concern about student loans, also known as "fence-sitters." LRAP stated about 70% of "fence-sitters" would not otherwise attend if not for LRAP. The additional populations we selected involved supporting students who may find LRAP helpful due to their relatively low starting salary and those who historically have higher borrowing rates and lack of family wealth.

In 2017, SPU's first-generation admits began to increase (over 30%) to levels that required targeted attention. First-generation students are often derailed from their education dreams due to a lack of information, fear of costs or that they "cannot make it," or the complicated processes of navigating college including financial options. Each year our admit pool consistently included high need students and 2017 was no different, with almost 26% of the admit pool eligible for the federal Pell Grant. Finally, in looking at programs with lower starting salaries, we decided to include theology majors in the LRAP offered population. So, our entire LRAP offer population was set: "fence-sitters," first-generation, Pell Grant recipients and theology majors.

So, our entire LRAP offer population was set: "fence-sitters," first-generation, Pell Grant recipients and theology majors.

In April 2017, Matt provided training on identifying students who expressed actual concern about student loans and how to work with them. The training also provided details of eligibility, how the program works post-graduation and our administrative setup. The activity was engaging, informative and persuasive. The staff were appreciative of the additional support of a new program. Now, we needed to figure out how to identify the students and communicate with them.

In 2017, the new Department of Enrollment Operations (EOPS) was also responsible for data in and out of the Admissions Administrative System/CRM. EOPS worked closely with Student Financial Services and Enrollment Communications to accurately code and communicate to students who were offered LRAP. We created codes for individual student nominations for LRAP (the "fence-sitters") and the population selections (first-generation, Pell recipients and theology majors). Once students were coded in the administrative system, we emailed the students to inform them about the LRAP offer, and EOPS would then submit the data to LRAP for communication. LRAP would message the student within 48 hours, pointing them to an SPU-LRAP portal to sign their offer. We had it set: the agreement, the populations, the training, the communication, the student portal and the receipt of the data from LRAP. Now, we wondered, would it work?

LRAP provided admissions counselors another touchpoint for students.

In 2017, our concerns for the deepening enrollment shortfall, changing demographics of the admit pool and data challenges were real. This challenge prompted SPU to launch a targeted LRAP campaign. LRAP would be offered to federal Pell Grant students, first-generation and/or theology majors, as well as students who had concerns about debt—"fence-sitters." Our goal was to increase enrollment with these efforts, knowing that LRAP was not a "fix-all" to shore up enrollment deficits. Our LRAP enrollment goal was 40 students.

We found within a few weeks of launching LRAP that it was resonating with some students. We surpassed our goal of enrolling 40 students with LRAP by eight at the end of April. LRAP provided Admissions Counselors another touchpoint for students. It offered them the opportunity to have lengthier discussions about college costs, demystify student loans and ultimately assuage real repayment fears. Additionally, with the federal parent PLUS loan covered by the program, parents could ease their minds a bit should their child be challenged in their job search. These parents, just 5+ years ago, came out of The Great Recession. The memories of foreclosures, income loss, decimation of home equity and unemployment were still fresh in their minds. And for some students in the targeted populations, their parents were often the most hard-hit by the economic downturn. LRAPs' safety-net was a welcome inclusion into their college cost calculus. It also provided us an additional value message we did not fully realize at the outset of implementation.

As a safety-net for low wages, LRAP is not something that

readily comes to mind as a program that speaks to the value of an institution's degree. A quick read without much deeper thinking could lead one to think, *Oh, Main Street University must offer this because their students are not as prepared as others. They must get low-paying jobs.* Yet, the actual message is the opposite.

With Matt's guidance and perspective, we began to talk about LRAP as a statement on the value of the SPU degree. Because SPU is investing in LRAP at no cost to the student, we believe an SPU degree will prepare students for the job market and financially cover their obligations. And if a student chooses a field with lower starting salaries or is impacted financially in the job market in some unforeseen way, LRAP is there to help. This reinforced that the SPU degree is valuable. We are investing further in your success. LRAP was part of the strength of our one-on-one discussions and led to victory. Additionally, we believed that caring for high-need students with LRAP complements our mission and differentiates us from similar schools.

Additionally, we believed that caring for high-need students with LRAP complements our mission and differentiates us from similar schools.

The goal to enroll 40 LRAP students was surpassed by the end of April 2017. By the Fall of 2017, SPU had 94 enrolled students who accepted the LRAP offer—over twice the projected number. We calculated that we needed just six LRAP students to attend who would not have otherwise done so to break even with the cost of LRAP. According to helpful survey results conducted by LRAP, 34 incoming freshmen enrolled because of LRAP! A total of 647 freshmen enrolled in 2017. Therefore, just over 5% of the freshman class was able to attend SPU because of LRAP. This was an incredible outcome.

Qualitatively, some of the students' comments about LRAP spoke to the power of relieving loan anxiety and why many of us work in higher education. The comments speak to the students' change in attitudes about student loans and their goals. With LRAP, students go from a scarcity mindset to one of opportunity— the attitude that makes university life full of energy, ideas and possibilities. Students who do not have a family member to guide them through the labyrinth of college processes and hurdles found that LRAP removed a significant barrier: "Seattle Pacific University Loan Repayment Assistance Program will make it possible for my family and me, due to our current income, to attend SPU and be the first of my family to earn a degree."

Additionally, LRAP provides students with the belief their future, post-graduation, is less burdened with debt's potential weight. It opens the door for students to attend schools they believe will support them to graduation. "The Seattle Pacific University loan repayment assistance program has allowed me to enroll at Seattle Pacific University without concern that I won't be able to pay back my loans. This opportunity has allowed me to be incredibly excited to attend such an amazing school and to be ready to succeed."

> **"LRAP has allowed me to be incredibly excited to attend such an amazing school and to be ready to succeed."**

The results in 2017 were considered a success. The entire SPU team worked doggedly to ensure the best freshman class as possible, given the challenges. We knew we would continue LRAP for the next year; the question was, should we expand the program and, if so, to whom?

The success of LRAP in 2017 gave us confidence in its impact on individual students, significantly lower-income students. In 2017, we had a battle on our hands to achieve a first-year student enrollment that was not devastating to our institutional budget. LRAP appears to have provided us with the students who would not have otherwise enrolled. The students were predominantly Pell Grant eligible and/or first in their family to attend college. We took this concept, offering LRAP to lower-income students, and expanded it in 2018.

Our data shows that when a parent borrows a federal parent PLUS loan, they typically borrow, annually, the Expected Family Contribution (EFC)—the calculation that the government expects an applicant's family to contribute to their annual college costs. The average EFC for our federal parent loan borrowers is about

$19,000, and 1 out of every 5 of our graduates received a parent loan. Most PLUS recipients are from incomes above, and sometimes barely above, Pell Grant eligibility. Middle-income students often have limited resources. They document some level of ability to pay for college but do not qualify for government grants. Beyond their family resources, scholarships, work and loans carry the cost load. Although we had a robust scholarship program, we believe LRAP was an answer for many of these students and low-income students.

The 2018 year was a banner year for our enrollment, and LRAP was a part of it. We increased scholarships and need-based institutional aid. In addition, we brought online a new admissions-based CRM. And we continued LRAP, expanding eligibility to students with AGIs equal to or less than $150,000. We believed this expansion would serve the middle-income students whose parents often borrowed federal PLUS loans.

By the Fall of 2017, SPU had 94 enrolled students who accepted the LRAP offer— over twice the projected number.

All the changes contributed to a stellar freshman enrollment of 714 students—the highest freshman enrollment in several years. We provided a total of 2,196 LRAP offers to admitted freshmen. We received 520 confirmed students who were offered LRAP, almost a 24% yield rate. The overall yield rate for 2018 was 19%. This was achieved in part due to an increasingly robust communication plan through the new CRM. Students were less confused about the process—what LRAP offered them or even if LRAP was a scam— and what they needed to do.

The enrollment team and the SPU community celebrated the freshman enrollment in 2018. It was as if the entire campus finally could exhale. The enrollment was welcome news, and in enrollment good news lasts only until the next enrollment cycle, which is never far away. So, we wanted to learn a bit more about what occurred in 2018.

After we unpacked the metrics of 2018, the freshman class was just a highly engaged group. The admitted pool completed a

FAFSA at a higher rate than any time before, 83%. They were more likely to be from in-state and had the highest number of visitors. In terms of LRAP, as I mentioned, the yield rate for students who were offered it (some accepted it, some did not) was higher than the overall yield rate. Yet, for those students who accepted the LRAP offer, the yield rate was slightly lower by about one percentage point. We still received wonderful comments from students. Yet, the data point of the yield of accepted LRAP offers began to raise questions of effectiveness.

The 2018 year was a banner year for our enrollment, and LRAP was part of it.

At the same time, we were concerned about the freshman discount rate (hard to name a school that is not concerned about this figure). For each year of offering LRAP, we have factored the LRAP per student fee into our awarding strategy, backing off institutional aid just a bit to help offset the cost of LRAP. The LRAP fee is charged to us for each student who accepts the offer, enrolls and borrows an eligible loan. Although it is a relatively lower cost to other endeavors, higher institutional aid, for example, remained a cost to our student aid budget. This impacted the discount rate. We were given the charge to curb the discount rate for the next year, 2019.

In 2019, we kept scholarships the same as the previous year, reduced some demographic scholarship amounts and changed the LRAP eligible population. In 2018, a student with a family AGI of $150,000 or less qualified to receive an LRAP Award. In 2019, merit students with an AGI of $100,000 or less and non-merit students with $150,000 or less qualified for an LRAP Award. This reduced our initial offers by about 150 students, not significant by any means, but it was part of our calculus to manage the discount rate.

What we found in 2019 was a return to enrollment behavior of the prior years. Students were less engaged than in 2018. FAFSA filing rates returned to previous levels of about 80%. The admit pool was more equally distributed between in-state and out-of-state students, and visits were the lowest of the prior three years. The efforts to curb the discount rate were met starkly with the realities of the class. We expanded scholarship offers and greatly expanded LRAP offers by offering them additional stale admits regardless of their income or merit award qualifications. The challenge to reduce the discount rate was insurmountable with the class behavior. Our final fall enrollment went from 714 in 2018 to 638 in 2019. And our discount rate continued to grow.

LRAP has been part of the answer to serving students, securing our enrollment and impacting our revenue.

As the cost to enroll a student continues to increase, the efficacy of LRAP will need to be demonstrated clearly and often. Thus far, we have found that retention of Fall 2018 to Fall 2019 LRAP recipients (79.3%) is essentially the same as the overall class (80%); it appears that LRAP did not impact their return. This data point will be reviewed closely in the next fall term. We do know students are positively affected, and at the same time, costs and effectiveness are critical measures.

Student comments and stories are useful on an anecdotal level and leave administrators feeling good about how the program positively affects students. Yet, the program's overall cost when offered to large swaths of an admit pool must be weighed against its effectiveness. Surveys reflect student sentiment that they would not enroll without the program and measure this attitude after receiving the program and its perceived benefits. It is like asking a kid who just had ice cream on a hot day, "Would you have felt as good without the ice cream?" After having it, one cannot imagine not having it and feeling so good. We would have liked to conduct a control test group to satisfy our need to understand the program's actual effectiveness. Still, that ship has sailed with our marketing and overall program eligible population. Additionally, once a program is fully launched, there is a risk in adjusting it so much to include a control group; the risk is that enrollment falls more because the program is effective.

Therefore, we continued with LRAP in 2020 and returned to the $150,000 AGI as a qualifying criterion to be offered with an

LRAP. We believe the program is beneficial for many students, and for some students, it does mean the difference in enrolling. With our competition of state schools and similar private institutions also offering LRAP, we feel compelled to continue to offer the program. So far, early 2020 results showed a return in a healthy yield rate of the class and a strong yield rate from students offered LRAP, including a more substantial yield rate for students who accepted the LRAP than the overall class.

LRAP is a vital tool that provides a safety-net for students in good and challenging economic times. LRAP is a vital tool that provides a safety-net for students in good and challenging economic times. LRAP helps us speak to our academic programs' strength and students' preparation for careers and supporting them in their calling. We continue to consider ways to fund the program and to manage the discount rate. The consequences of financial questions in difficult budgetary times may end up winning the day. If stiff competition remains, the value of an education is seen primarily through an economic lens, and students and families remain concerned about debt, LRAP will have a significant role to play with our financial aid services for students. Without a comprehensive and specific answer to student (and parent) debt, schools must mitigate student borrowing through decreased college costs in a cost-increasing world or increase financial aid in a budget-tightening reality. LRAP has been part of the answer to serving students, securing our enrollment and impacting our revenue. Students often cut to the core of our purpose in increasing access to higher education, and LRAP students are no different. This is from a 2020 LRAP recipient:

"When looking for a college to attend, I didn't have any options that did not include my taking out lots of loans. I was beginning to think I wasn't going to move into higher education. When I received notice of this program, a huge weight was lifted off me."

CHAPTER 14

OVERCOMING SKEPTICISM

SEAN-MICHAEL GREEN
ALBERTUS MAGNUS COLLEGE

L et's start this narrative with a confession: I am a bit cynical. I look for the fine print or the catch in any deal. Anything that seems too good to be true raises my hackles. I can smell a salesperson from a mile away, and I am more or less immune to gimmicks.

This disposition suited me well as a Vice President for Enrollment Management.

My institution was Albertus Magnus College—the second most prestigious private school in New Haven, Connecticut. Although Yale was our neighbor, they were not a serious competitor. Our region, however, was saturated with colleges and universities. The University of Connecticut system and the state universities offered a variety of majors, a lower sticker price and a name brand that was hard to match. To make matters more challenging, we were also competing with many private colleges and universities. In this crowded environment, each school developed and honed its unique identity.

ABOUT THE AUTHOR: Sean-Michael Green is the Vice President of Client Service at Ardeo Education Solutions. He is the former Vice President for Enrollment Management at Albertus Magnus College. After serving in the United States Marine Corps, he earned his bachelor's degree at the University of Pittsburgh. He holds graduate degrees from Marist College, the University of Pennsylvania and Cornell University.

Our identity was composed of three parts. Albertus Magnus was a Catholic college in the Dominican tradition. St. Dominic's followers adhere to four pillars: study, service, community and prayer. And those pillars became the cornerstones to which we tied many of our actions. This helped us to clarify the experience of an Albertus Magnus education. Secondly, we had few students. When I arrived in 2017, we brought in just over 100 new students each fall to contribute to a traditional undergraduate population of 500 students. If you wanted an intimate undergraduate education, Albertus Magnus was your choice. Finally, we were a school that served a high-need population. We had the highest percentage of Pell-eligible students for any private school in the state, at 59% of our student population.

In six instances, we successfully used LRAP in this way that summer.

Before I joined the school, our CFO signed an agreement with LRAP Association, now Ardeo Education Solutions. I inherited the relationship upon my arrival. I was intrigued by the concept of an LRAP, but I was skeptical. They sounded great, and I checked some references for the company, but I wasn't ready to dive in.

Rather, I dipped in a toe. Over my first summer, an incoming student reached out to a team member to say that she would not enroll in the fall. Her family was reluctant to take out a Parent Plus loan. We offered the promise of an LRAP: If upon graduating, she did not earn a sufficient salary, we would help her repay her student loans. Her family was thrilled, and she was able to attend Albertus Magnus, her first-choice school. In six instances, we successfully used LRAP in this way that summer. Out of an incoming group of 108 students, six of them attended because we could serve those families with an LRAP.

We used it in a more significant way the following year. It became part of our financial aid appeals process. We had a budget set aside to sweeten the pot for students who needed a bit more money to enroll with us. The appeals process always seemed to be beneath the dignity of the life-changing investment we were discussing. If a family had a concern that could be resolved with a few thousand dollars in additional discount, it seemed that either the concern was not severe or the remedy was inadequate. We used LRAPs to change the conversation. It was no longer about what one school was offering compared to our offer; it was about our commitment to ensuring a positive outcome for the student. We did not offer additional discounts, but we offered the promise of an LRAP; with this approach, we saved and enrolled 20 incoming students who submitted an appeal.

> **We used LRAPs to change the conversation. It was no longer about what one school was offering compared to our offer; it was about our commitment to ensuring a positive outcome for the student.**

I finally accelerated my use of the tool in my third year. If you were a high-academic performer applying to Albertus Magnus, you could expect an invitation to our Honors Program. If you were at the other end of the academic spectrum but earned admission, we offered you plenty of remedial help. Similarly, a student from a family with plenty of financial need had Pell and state aid programs; and those from more affluent backgrounds were often seduced with more institutional aid. The middle of the class, however, had no special programs or incentives. I filled this gap with LRAP.

Make no mistake, we pulled other levers as well. We added athletic teams, expanded our outreach and promoted new majors. LRAP was one ingredient in a complicated recipe. But we grew our incoming class to more than 280 new students, 52 of whom enrolled with the protection of an LRAP.

How was my cynical nature tamed?

I suppose the first assault on it was simply the results LRAP produced. It helped me to achieve my goals on a small scale—such as allowing a frightened family to suspend their disbelief and attend my institution; and it also helped on a large scale—such as contributing to the largest incoming class in the history of the school. It was hard to remain distrustful with such excellent outcomes.

The second factor—and I am a bit embarrassed to admit this—

was the quality of the people I met at Ardeo. My point of contact was a former Vice President for Enrollment who understood my challenges. He was not a one-dimensional character shoveling LRAPs my way but rather a professional colleague. He invited me to a client event where I met with other schools using LRAPs as well as his company colleagues. Ardeo was a community of smart and driven people, and frankly, I wanted to be part of it. I lowered my defenses in the face of such unrelenting camaraderie.

A final influential factor was the control I had over the tool. At no time did I feel any pressure to use LRAPs in any particular way. I determined how many offers we would make and to whom we would make them. We only paid when the offer resulted in a student who enrolled and borrowed. There were never any other fees. If it worked, I paid a predictable amount; if it didn't work to bring in the student, I didn't pay. This meant that I saw an immediate return on investment with every dollar I spent. In my years in higher education, I never experienced a vendor like this.

> **In my years in higher education, I never experienced a vendor like this.**

In the end, I left Albertus Magnus and joined the team at Ardeo. My role is to help people understand the tool's impact and the control they have over it. I speak to Vice Presidents for Enrollment Management at private schools in New England every day. As you might imagine, I face a great deal of cynicism.

My relationship with karma aside, my role at Ardeo provides me with an opportunity to help my colleagues in the industry and to help the families that benefit from the protection of an LRAP. It is a rewarding way to serve the profession, and it is even more interesting because of its unlikely beginning.

CHAPTER 15

THE PLU PLEDGE: A BOLD INVESTMENT IN THE FUTURE OF OUR STUDENTS

MIKE FRECHETTE
PACIFIC LUTHERAN UNIVERSITY

I n the Fall of 2017, I found myself sitting in a conference room with our marketing and enrollment teams brainstorming synonyms for the word "promise." This wasn't exactly the typical Tuesday afternoon for a Dean of Enrollment Management. We had just signed a contract with Ardeo Education Solutions to provide Loan Repayment Assistance Programs (LRAPs) to all incoming freshmen. We were working on a private label name for our LRAP program. We landed on the PLU Pledge, which I still like. It's simple but effective. The PLU Pledge is a powerful promise to our students, guaranteeing that a Pacific Lutheran University degree is worth it.

We tried two other LRAP strategies before adopting the one we currently use. Sometimes it takes experimenting to find the right strategy that works best for you and your student body. Results

---

ABOUT THE AUTHOR: Mike Frechette serves as the Dean of Enrollment Management and Student Financial Services at Pacific Lutheran University. He has worked in higher education for more than 15 years and is passionate about creating educational access for students and their families. Mike holds a bachelor's degree from Boston University and a master's degree from the University of Chicago.

were sometimes mixed, but we believe LRAP has significantly helped our University enroll more students while offering real value. Before we get too deep into the details about how Pacific Lutheran University uses LRAP, let me tell you a little about PLU to assist you in identifying similarities and differences between your institution and mine.

Pacific Lutheran University is located in the beautiful Pacific Northwest in Parkland, Washington, a small community just south of Washington's second-largest city, Tacoma. Founded in 1890 by Norwegian immigrants, PLU maintains its close affiliation with the Evangelic Lutheran Church of America. It's the closest college to Mount Rainier, and the physical campus resides on the traditional lands of the Nisqually, Puyallup, Squaxin Island and Steilacoom peoples. PLU has approximately 3,100 students, 360 of whom are graduate students. Like many small liberal arts colleges, PLU intentionally combines liberal arts and professional studies. The University consistently ranks among the top universities in the West and is well-known for its nursing, fine arts, kinesiology and education programs.

> **LRAP has significantly helped our University enroll more students while offering real value.**

Global education is a distinguishing feature of the PLU experience, with nearly half of all students challenging their perspectives by studying away at some point during their academic career. PLU's study away program is nationally recognized, and we were the first school to have students studying away on all seven continents simultaneously. Almost 20% of students cite it as one of the top three reasons for attending PLU.

Pacific Lutheran University is decidedly a regional institution, drawing 75% of its enrollment from Washington state. Nevertheless, there is a critical mass of students who travel from their homes in states such as Hawaii, Oregon, Nevada, Alaska, Colorado and Minnesota to attend PLU. There is also a small contingent of international students—anywhere from 50 to 100—on campus each year, many of whom come from Norway. This is a unique feature of PLU's international enrollment.

As America's graduating high school seniors' demographic has changed, so too has the makeup of PLU's incoming classes. In recent years, the institution has welcomed incoming classes with over 40% students of color and 40% first-generation students. The institution recently became a member of the Hispanic Association of Colleges and Universities to recognize that over 10% of the total student body self-identifies as Hispanic. In the Fall of 2019, 1 in 3 incoming students were Pell-eligible, and many more were just outside of Pell range. Over 90% of students received some form of financial aid. PLU's generous financial aid packages are consistently cited as one of the top reasons students decide to attend the University. According to LendEDU, PLU is the best college in Washington for financial aid, and we are ranked ninth nationally according to lendedu.com/blog/best-colleges-for-financial-aid-in-2020/

> **The PLU Pledge is a powerful promise to our students, guaranteeing that a Pacific Lutheran University degree is worth it.**

Washington is a state with a well-supported and strong public higher education system, and for this reason, the public institutions in the state tend to control the market. The University of Washington is one of the most prestigious schools in the country. Even smaller public institutions such as Western Washington University and Washington State University are a big draw for the state's graduating high school seniors each year. The state's public institutions' strength makes them very visible within the prospective student market and an obvious first choice. For this reason, the small private schools in Washington, such as PLU, must market themselves very cleverly and aggressively to emerge from the shadows of the towering publics.

The state of Washington also heavily subsidizes higher education, which keeps tuition at public institutions relatively low. Furthermore, Washington has one of the most progressive and generous state grant programs in the entire country. The Washington College Grant covers the full tuition of many students at the state's public institutions. To remain competitive, Washington's private colleges and universities offer steep discount rates to avoid being completely outpriced by the state's public institutions. In other words, financial aid and other financial incentives are powerful recruitment tools for private institutions in the state of Washington.

The Fall 2016 semester at PLU arrived with a new record for the 21st century—not the type you want to set. Since the start of the millennium, the lowest first fall to second fall retention rate was in 2001 at 80.6% until 2016, when it dipped to 79%. Though we were still well above the national average, PLU's average retention rate typically hovers in the low 80s, and in Fall 2015, it was 82.8%. A drop in retention of close to 4% resulted in an immediate financial impact for a tuition-dependent institution. The Provost at the time was brand new, and she called for a renewed campus effort from all corners of the University to improve retention through comprehensive data analysis and to generate ideas to enhance student success. The data took several months to pull, and to be honest, it did not reveal a single reason why retention dropped below average heading into the Fall of 2016. Historically, several factors have contributed to PLU's retention rate: no direct admission to the School of Nursing, the challenge of incorporating commuter students into the life of the campus, and the inability of some students to work on campus and find community. For whatever reason, the myriad of factors contributing to the retention rate at PLU seemed to be amplified for the cohort that started in the Fall of 2015.

When I first learned about LRAPs, I immediately saw the value and novelty in offering this kind of safety-net to students increasingly concerned with student loan debt.

Nevertheless, the campus adopted several best practices to ensure that future retention rates did not experience such an unsustainable decline. We began offering housing discounts to low-income students living within a 25-mile radius of campus. We secured donations to provide additional gift aid to two groups with noticeably low retention: independent students due to exceptional circumstances and students whose parents were denied a parent loan. In a major decision, the Provost restructured Enrollment Services into Enrollment Management, moving from a Division that included Admission and Financial Aid to one that also included the Registrar and Academic Advising. This move provided the University with a structure to generate new enrollment and strategically plan to bolster and improve retention.

Students and families increasingly question the value of a college education and experience severe anxiety over accumulating debt. This reality drives home the need for a tool like LRAP.

Shortly after restructuring the Enrollment Department, the Provost asked me to serve as Dean of Enrollment Management, giving me the ability to seriously examine using a yield tool I'd explored at my last institution but hadn't used. When I first learned about LRAPs, I immediately saw the value and novelty in offering this kind of safety-net to students increasingly concerned with student loan debt. Several years ago, I recalled listening to an incoming student talking with someone at our front desk, insisting that she would not borrow student loans under any circumstances. While that's just one example, it is consistent with national data showing that while aggregate student loan debt is increasing, the average annual amount borrowed per undergraduate student decreases, according to research.collegeboard.org/pdf/trends-college-pricing-student-aid-2020.pdf. These statistics suggest that students and families increasingly question the value of a college education and experience severe anxiety over accumulating debt. This reality drives home the need for a tool like LRAP.

Therefore, I was happy that when I discussed LRAPs with PLU's Provost in the Winter of 2017, she was intrigued by the product and thought if we offered it on a case-by-case basis, it could improve retention. Many students facing financial hardship do not borrow, and a product like an LRAP can boost confidence in borrowing and allow students to persist. Furthermore, offering LRAP to students in danger of withdrawing is relatively low risk. If you offer LRAP to an at-risk student and the student matriculates, you have fulfilled your institutional mission while receiving net-tuition revenue from the student. If the student does not stay, there is no added cost to the school or student.

To be honest, very few students who contemplated leaving PLU decided to stay because of LRAP; however, timing may have had something to do with this. Many first-year students who withdraw from PLU do so during or after their first term. Those who enroll for a second term often do so knowing they will not return for the following academic year. By the time we signed with Ardeo, we were offering LRAP late in the academic year, which, we concluded, may have prevented us from achieving our desired result. The attractiveness of an LRAP was simply not enough for students whose academic performance was acutely suffering or for those students who had already made up their minds about transferring. Nevertheless, our retention rate improved, heading into the Fall of 2017, and it has stayed north of 80% since that time (with the exception of a small decline in 2020 due to the pandemic.)

For PLU, deposit activity so far after May 1 proved that LRAP gives students and families the confidence they need to attend our institution. Our experience using the stale funnel approach led to more serious conversations that summer about expanding our use of the product and marketing it broadly to our prospective students and families.

As the Spring 2017 semester came to an end, the University's attention quickly turned to yield season. In the Fall of 2016, we welcomed 678 new first-year students to campus, and when May 1, 2017 arrived, we found ourselves 40 deposits down from this number. The Associate Dean of Admissions and I began discussing some late-in-the-game strategies to yield more deposits, and we wondered if LRAP could assist in this regard. When I reached out to Ardeo, their team advised me on the "stale funnel" approach.

The "stale funnel" approach is perhaps the lowest-risk approach to utilizing LRAP as a recruitment tool. As most enrollment folks know, post-May 1 deposits are minimal, so offering LRAP to all pending deposits after May 1 (i.e., the stale funnel) carries little financial risk. Any additional deposits a school can yield with this approach are a bonus. When we explained this idea to our Provost and CFO, they immediately recognized this approach as a low-risk, no-brainer. If we yielded additional deposits by offering LRAP, great. If not, then there was no cost to PLU or the student. In late May of that year, we offered LRAP to all of our admitted first-year students who had not deposited at PLU or had withdrawn their admission application. Almost immediately, six students deposited and attended PLU in the fall. For PLU, deposit activity so far after May 1 proved that LRAP gives students and families the confidence they need to attend our institution. Our experience using the stale funnel approach led to more serious conversations that summer about expanding our use of the product and marketing it broadly to our prospective students and families.

What could better demonstrate care for our students than providing them with loan repayment assistance at no cost to them upon graduating from the University?

Offering LRAP to a large population of the incoming student body is a significant investment. It required a level of thoughtfulness and calculation that was unnecessary when using LRAPs as a lower-risk retention tool. Because of the investment required, I know many enrollment leaders struggle to win over Presidents, CFOs and Provosts who are understandably concerned about budgets, especially during a time of challenging demographic changes. In the Summer of 2017, the stars seemed to align for PLU. First, we were in the midst of a Presidential transition. A former CFO was named interim President which might spell doom for many enrollment managers when providing new financial incentives to prospective students. As many of us know, there are two basic types of CFOs—bean counters and investors—and our President was most certainly among the latter category. We had a Fall 2017 incoming class of 619, 59 fewer students from the Fall of 2016. Our President was ready to invest in some new recruitment strategies.

Ardeo's team was instrumental in helping us realize how LRAP could fit into our recruitment plan for the upcoming admission season. First, LRAP is completely mission-aligned. Everything PLU does is mission-driven: "PLU seeks to educate students for lives of thoughtful inquiry, service, leadership and care—for other people, for their communities and for the Earth." What could better demonstrate care for our students than providing them with loan repayment assistance at no cost to them upon graduating from the University? Second, Ardeo showed us how we could invest wisely. Since PLU has no trouble attracting nursing students to its strong program and graduating nurses almost always earn a salary that makes them ineligible to receive loan repayment assistance, it didn't make sense to provide them with LRAP. After crunching some numbers, Ardeo's team showed us we would need to enroll about 25 additional non-nursing students next fall to pay for the cost of providing LRAP to all non-nursing students. This goal seemed very achievable for us. Given the new President's eagerness to invest in recruitment, the decision to move forward with an expanded Ardeo contract was an easy one for PLU.

> **Ardeo provides its clients with marketing support by reaching out to students and parents through phone calls, emails and digital marketing on behalf of their clients.**

In the first year of our newly expanded contract with Ardeo, we decided to automatically provide LRAP to all incoming freshmen except for nursing students. As a retention tool, we decided to provide LRAPs to nursing students who leave the nursing program before their sophomore year. By the time we finalized our decision, the fall semester had already started which did not leave a lot of time to ramp up our marketing efforts. It might seem obvious, but strong and effective marketing is key to reaping the enrollment benefits of LRAP. If prospective students and parents are unaware of the product, it will not function as a useful recruitment and yield tool. Our Admission and Marketing teams partnered, and within a couple of hours, we had branded our LRAP and brainstormed ideas for a website, postcard and press release. Ardeo provides its clients with marketing support by reaching out to students and parents through phone calls, emails and digital marketing on behalf of their clients. Our combined marketing efforts were received well by prospective students and families, and despite the late start in our first-year marketing LRAP broadly, we yielded some promising results. While we welcomed a relatively small class of 619 in the Fall of 2017, we welcomed a class of 649 in the Fall of 2018. In short, we yielded enough additional students to cover the cost of providing LRAP to all of our incoming non-nursing students. However, the growth we experienced was exclusively in nursing students, which complicates our results. In the Fall of 2017, 520 of our incoming students were non-nursing students, and in the Fall of 2018, 517 incoming students were non-nursing students.

The PLU Pledge—our LRAP private label name—was a top-three reason for choosing to attend PLU.

While these results suggest that providing LRAP was not an effective recruitment tool, other metrics highlight its success. In May of 2018, we implemented a deposit survey, in which we asked incoming students for the top three reasons why they decided to deposit at PLU. Of 263 respondents, 8.7% indicated that the PLU Pledge—our LRAP private label name—was a top-three reason for choosing to attend PLU. In addition, a third-party company conducted parent research for us. Of the matriculant parents who responded to the survey, 14% said the PLU Pledge made it possible for their students to attend.

Regarding the Fall 2018 class makeup, PLU experienced an increase in students of color from 38% the previous fall to 45%. This growth in students of color was fueled by additional students who self-identify as Hispanic, a demographic shift among graduating high school students in Washington and the rest of the country. I do not have any data to show this shift was directly due to the PLU Pledge. In fact, the students who indicated in our deposit survey that the PLU Pledge drove their decision to attend PLU came from a wide variety of socio-economic backgrounds. Nevertheless, a surge in students of color during our first year of providing LRAP to almost all students might not be entirely coincidental. As we have continued to offer the PLU Pledge to all non-nursing students over the last few years, our student of color ratio has held steady at 45%.

Although results were mixed upon our first year of providing LRAP to almost all students, there were enough positive indicators to renew for a second year, especially since we had a late start on our marketing efforts the previous fall. We doubled down on our awareness strategies, mentioning the PLU Pledge in every presentation and also in a letter sent from me in the early fall to all prospective students' families in our inquiry pool. Furthermore, we decided to take advantage of a new strategy Ardeo began offering that year—offer to all. While LRAP is an enticing benefit for many families, some families are completely confident they will not borrow. As a result, they are not motivated to attend by the PLU Pledge. By offering the PLU Pledge to all non-nursing students instead of automatically providing, we asked students to opt-in, ensuring we were not paying for students who were not motivated by LRAP.

> **Possessing a distinctive advantage is critical to enrollment success today, which is why our President decided to sign another two-year contract with Ardeo after Fall 2019.**

Some on campus were worried about this approach, thinking students would overlook our messaging and not realize they had to opt into the PLU Pledge for Fall 2019. However, over 70% of eligible students opted in. Like many schools in the Fall of 2019, we welcomed a much smaller class of 597 students, 491 non-nursing. However, according to our deposit survey for the Fall 2019 class, 15% cited the PLU Pledge as one of their top three reasons for attending, which is almost double from the previous year. This figure clearly indicates that our earlier messaging and experience explaining the program helped us convince students and families that LRAP is a powerful, unique benefit. According to the Ardeo-sponsored third-party research for the Fall 2019 class, 31% of respondents said their child would not be attending PLU without the PLU Pledge. In other words, although our incoming class was smaller than the previous year, these data points show it might have been even smaller if it were not for the PLU Pledge.

In the recent past, any financial incentive goal was to yield enough additional students to at least cover the cost of offering the incentive. In today's enrollment environment of unprecedented demographic challenges (and a global pandemic), the question is not: "How many students will I gain by offering a particular financial incentive?" The question is: "How many students will I lose if I don't?" Possessing a distinctive advantage is critical to enrollment success today which is why our President decided to sign another two-year contract with Ardeo after Fall 2019. By signing a two-year contract, we can now start marketing to juniors and provide even earlier messaging about the benefits of attending a school like PLU that offers LRAP. We even offered the PLU Pledge to students looking to transfer from a nearby private school that had recently closed. In part due to the PLU Pledge, 23 of these students will be transferring to PLU for their next academic year, 9 of whom are non-nursing.

Ardeo's team was instrumental in helping us realize how LRAP could fit into our recruitment plan for the upcoming admission season.

Offering LRAP as broadly as PLU does is a significant investment. Fortunately, our President is committed to investing boldly in the initiatives that give PLU a competitive advantage. For those of you with Presidents and CFOs who are more hesitant about this type of investment, it is important to note there are ways to use LRAP that are relatively low-risk, as I've discussed in this chapter. We are looking forward to hearing our first beneficiaries' stories and how the PLU Pledge allowed them to pursue a job based on their passion and not just the starting salary. It will be useful to see data on the graduates who benefit the most from the PLU Pledge. What did they study? Where are they working now? Answers to these questions will help us become even more targeted in our use of the PLU Pledge in the future.

A POWERFUL PROMISE FULFILLED

I magine being able to make this promise to your students: If your income after graduation is modest, we will help you repay your student and parent loans! Ardeo Education Solutions helps colleges and universities make this powerful promise to students.

By providing a guarantee their degree will pay off, LRAPs give students the confidence to follow their dreams. More than 20,000 students have benefited from LRAP:

- It has helped them attend their first-choice college.
- It has encouraged them to persist and complete their degree.
- It has empowered them to pursue their passions rather than a paycheck.

Many students and families today question the long-term value of a college degree, which only continues to increase the competitive market in which colleges across the country find themselves. More than 200 colleges and universities have used LRAPs to advance their institutional goals:

- It has helped them make college more accessible to chronically disadvantaged students.
- It has enhanced their brand, signaling to students that they care about what happens to them post-graduation.
- It has helped them increase their enrollment and net-tuition revenue.

We know college is worth it. We are proud to work with hundreds of institutions across the United States to make a degree possible for so many. Ardeo Education Solutions' powerful promise is not just a practical solution to a pervasive problem. It is also a beacon of hope for many students and families who feel a college degree is simply out of reach.

Since 2008, we have partnered with colleges and universities to eliminate the fear surrounding student loan debt and reinforce a commitment to student success and graduate outcomes. We are proud to partner with institutions across diverse segments of higher education, at both small colleges and large universities, in nearly every region of the country—all fulfilling the powerful promise of LRAP!

You may be at the end of this book, but we hope the stories within these pages—told by college Administrators and students— have inspired you. We hope that in reaching the end, you have also reached a beginning.

If you are interested in learning more about partnering with Ardeo Education Solutions and discovering how LRAPs can help your institution, please visit ardeoeducation.org/get-started or send a message to Peter@ardeoeducation.org to reach out to our President directly.

Made in the USA
Monee, IL
14 October 2021